Not I, But Christ

Corrie ten Boom

NOT I, BUT CHRIST

THOMAS NELSON PUBLISHERS
Nashville • Camden • New York

Original title *Niet ik, maar Christus*

The jacket photograph and the photograph on page 8 are by Russ Busby.

Book and jacket design by Nancy Bozeman

Published in Nashville, Tennessee, by Thomas Nelson, Inc. and distributed in Canada by Lawson Falle, Ltd., Cambridge, Ontario.

Printed in the United States of America.

All Scripture quotations in this publication are from the King James Version of the Bible.

Library of Congress Cataloging in Publication Data

Ten Boom, Corrie.
Not I, but Christ.

1. Christian life — 1960- — Addresses, essays, lectures. I. Title.
BV4501.2.T383 1983 248.4 84-1965
ISBN 0-8407-4112-X

Title page photo: Basel, Switzerland

Contents

Publisher's Preface

N*ot I, But Christ* is a perfect summation of the life of an extraordinary woman, Corrie ten Boom. It was her wish always to magnify and exalt her Lord Jesus Christ. Because of Corrie's single-minded devotion to Christ, we are proud to publish this book, and we hope and pray that it, too, will help to accomplish that work to which Corrie gave her life.

Most of the text of this book comes from a series of radio messages Corrie delivered in Dutch over Trans World Radio in the late 1960s. Originally published in Dutch (under the title *Niet ik, maar Christus*) in a different format, this is the first English translation of these talks, prepared by Lotte Reimeringer, long-time coworker with Corrie. A few of the messages were gleaned from Corrie's magazine, *The Hiding Place.*

Growing out of Corrie's great love for God was a love for people and for the beauty of the earth He created. Accordingly, some of the photographs in this book feature Corrie with people she met in her travels around the world, and some are of Corrie's favorite scenic pictures that she took herself.

Foreword

"When somebody is eighty-four years of age and is still able to do just a little bit of the work she loves, that is a great privilege; but I am able to do so much!" Those were Corrie ten Boom's words at the beginning of our seven-year working relationship in 1976. She was continually thankful to God that she was able to reach many people with the gospel of the Lord Jesus Christ, and she went about her task with an enthusiasm I have never seen equaled. As we traveled through several countries, including the United States, she made the most of every opportunity, particularly emphasizing the need to forgive our enemies in the power of the Lord Jesus and to be ready for Jesus' coming again.

Tante Corrie saw life very simply. She spoke to the Lord constantly. She said that God had no problems, only plans. She accepted the fame that her books and films brought her simply as a platform from which to address an even larger number of people. When she was personally complimented she would say that Corrie ten Boom in herself was nobody—the Lord Jesus was the one to whom her admirers should look, and whom they should follow and obey. "He hath made him to be sin for us, who knew no sin; that we might be made the righteousness of God in him," she would tell them, quoting from 2 Corinthians 5:21. She would quote these words of an anonymous poet:

Cowardly, wayward, and weak
I change with the changing sky.
Today so eager and strong
Tomorrow not caring to try.
But He never gives in,
And we two shall win,
Jesus and I.

In her heart she would accept each compliment as if it were a flower. At the end of the day she would raise the "bouquet" of flowers to the Lord and say, "It is all Yours, Lord!"

How she enjoyed life. This master communicator was full of unconditional love, which she would extend to old and young, rich and poor, prisoner and monarch, black and white. And what a sense of humor she had! We spent a lot of time laughing; she was very young in spirit. Her days included traveling; writing; counseling; speaking; and conducting interviews for the press, radio, and television.

In 1977, Tante Corrie moved into her own home in Placentia, California, near Los Angeles. Happy to sleep in the same bed every night, she no longer led the life of a "tramp for the Lord." But she did not slow down in the fulfillment of her life's calling. In fact she worked with even more urgency on the completion of several films and books. Looking back, one can see a reason for the sense of urgency: On August 23, 1978, Tante Corrie suffered a severe stroke which rendered her mute.

So began a life chapter with many important lessons for those of us who were privileged to serve her. Successive strokes caused paralysis, and for the last part of her life she was unable to leave her bed. Though she became extremely weak physically, spiritually, it seemed she was even stronger.

She could not speak, read, or write, but we learned to communicate in other ways. Despite the fact it was sometimes very difficult for her, she accepted her physical limitations and drew her strength from the Word of God, and from the Lord Himself, with whom she still constantly communed.

It sometimes required creativity to discover what she wanted to know. When we had tried for a long time to discover that which normally would have been communicated in a few seconds, we would say, "Let's ask the Lord." It can truly be said that in 90 percent of the cases we knew the answer within the next couple of minutes. We would then rejoice about the accomplished communication, meet the need, if there was one, and wonder why we do not go to the Lord sooner with all our questions, large and small. During those years of great weakness, the fruit of the Holy Spirit was very evident in Tante Corrie's life. Every visitor would comment on the overriding sense of the peace of God in the house, and she persevered with joy and patience.

We drew much comfort from the Psalms. Psalm 27 was one we read often, encouraging each other to wait for the Lord—it was often not easy in the midst of great physical hardship. On April 15, 1983, her ninety-first birthday, the Lord Jesus took Tante Corrie home. That afternoon we had sung to her, told her that nothing could ever separate her from the love of God, and said that the Lord was coming for her soon. At 11:00 P.M. she went to Him, very quietly and peacefully, her work accomplished. She had served Jesus Christ in her strength; she served Him in her weakness. She served Him in her life; she served Him in her death. How precious her life and testimony were to Him, even when she was removed from the public eye. She followed and obeyed Him then as consistently as she ever had.

You will have noticed that we, who were so close to her, can only describe Corrie ten Boom in what may seem to be glowing terms. In her own autobiographies, which many of you have read, she very honestly discloses her own faults, failings, and sins and how the Lord dealt with them and her. The impression we want to pass on is this: Every lesson she ever taught us—"Jesus is Victor"; "There is no pit so deep that He is not deeper still"—was fully tested during the last years of her life. And they all stood the test victoriously. Seeing her life, one saw the Lord Jesus Christ and wanted to be more like Him.

PAM ROSEWELL

Not I, But Christ

Holland

Holland

one

WHAT IS A CHRISTIAN'S CALLING?

In what kind of world are we living? Reading the newspapers and listening to the news sometimes cause me to feel desperate and hopeless. We cannot see the end of it all. We become afraid and ask ourselves where it is leading.

What a comfort it is to read the Bible and to see that God has known for a long, long time everything that is happening now and that He promises us a wonderful future straight through all the dreadful happenings.

The Lord Jesus speaks in His farewell in Luke 21 of the things we now can read in the newspapers.

That hard-to-understand book of Revelation is now clearer than it was ten or twenty years ago. In that book we read of dreadful things that we can expect, but John wrote from the divine perspective.

In chapter 21, verse 4, he says: "God shall wipe away all tears from their eyes; and there shall be no more death, neither sorrow, nor crying, neither shall there be any more pain: for the former things are passed away."

When we read the news we say: "The worst is still to come."

When we read the Bible, we can say joyfully: "The best is yet to be!"

Jesus promised He will make all things new (see Rev. 21:5). Then this earth, this dark earth, will be covered with the knowledge of the Lord, as the waters cover the bottom of the sea.

When reading God's blueprint of world history, we receive the safe knowledge that God has plans with this world.

The Lord Jesus warned about watching for the signs of the times (see Matt. 16:3). And if we do so, we shall notice that He will return very soon.

How can we be ready? By surrendering to Him, of whom Paul said, "Being confident of this very thing, that he which hath begun a good work in you will perform it until the day of Jesus Christ" (Phil. 1:6).

From this we see that we must not fight, but surrender to the Lord Jesus so He can prepare us for His return.

In 1 Thessalonians we read: "And the very God of peace sanctify you wholly; and . . . your whole spirit and soul and body be preserved blameless unto the coming of our Lord Jesus Christ. Faithful is he that calleth you, who also will do it" (5:23–24).

Just think what it means: You and I are blameless in soul and body. And it is possible because He, who calls you, is faithful. And He "also will do it."

When Jesus speaks of our days, He says: "And it shall turn to you for a testimony. . . . I will give you a mouth and wisdom, which all your adversaries shall not be able to gainsay nor resist. . . . there shall not an hair of your head perish. . . . And when these things begin to come to pass, then look up, and lift up your heads; for your redemption draweth nigh" (Luke 21:13, 15, 18, 28).

Jesus said, "Behold, I make all things new" (Rev. 21:5).

What riches, for you and for me! And even if things get worse, the best is yet to be!

Lord Jesus, come quickly and do what You promised — make all things new! And for these days, we pray, comfort us and grant us the wonderful experience to pass on this comfort to others. Thank You, Lord. Amen.

two

WHAT MUST I DO WITH MY SINS?

Dear fellow sinners, I have a message for you. The devil is like a good cattle dealer who walks once around a cow and then knows all its weak spots. He knows us and knows exactly where he can hit us. The devil has not yet retired. He knows that his time is short, and he is extremely active.

But Jesus is present, much stronger than the devil.

And this is exactly the answer to our sin problem. Jesus says in Matthew 9:13, "I am not come to call the righteous, but sinners to repentance."

But what must we do? In Proverbs 28:13 we read, "He that covereth his sins shall not prosper: but whoso confesseth and forsaketh them shall have mercy."

And John says, "If we confess our sins, he is faithful and just to forgive us our sins, and to cleanse us from all unrighteousness" (1 John 1:9).

Once a man went to the village priest to confess his sins and receive absolution. He said: "I stole three sacks of potatoes." The priest listened and pointed to repentance and forgiveness.

When they had finished talking, the priest said: "I heard about that theft, but thought only two sacks were taken. You spoke of three."

"Yes," the man answered, "but tomorrow I am going to steal the third one."

Who confesses his sins and stops sinning? Jesus revealed, as never before, His great mercy toward sinners in the case of the woman taken in adultery. He said: "He that is without sin among you, let him first cast a stone at her" (John 8:7). All to whom He said this went away. Then the Lord said to the sinful woman: "Go, and sin no more" (John 8:11).

Perhaps you will say: "That sounds very pleasant that the Lord says, 'Sin no more.' To me that is like a high mountaintop on which I shall never be able to stand."

Do you know what is so wonderful? When you start climbing with the Lord Jesus, you will see that it is a plateau, not a peak, and you will experience the truth of Psalm 18:36 where a sinner says to the Lord: "Thou hast enlarged my steps under me." The Bible speaks simply.

"Only acknowledge thine iniquity, that thou hast transgressed against the LORD thy God" (Jer. 3:13). And the wonderful words: "Come now, and let us reason together, saith the LORD: though your sins be as scarlet, they shall be as white as snow; though they be red like crimson, they shall be as wool" (Is. 1:18).

Jesus died on the cross to set sinners free. He or she whom Jesus sets free, is free indeed.

When the devil shows us our sins, he does so in order to make us desperate. "This is what you are," he says, "and you will stay like that all your life."

When the Holy Spirit shows us our sins, it is always in the light of the finished work on the cross. There Jesus died for you and for me. And He did not only die for us, He lives and He is always with us.

A little three-year-old boy met his father at the station. "I want to carry your suitcase, Daddy."

"All right, boy," the father said, "put your hand on mine."

So they carried the heavy suitcase home, where the boy said to his mommy: "I carried Daddy's suitcase."

This is just what we must do: Put our weak hand in Jesus' strong hand. Then we shall be strong together with Him—yes, more than conquerors. You and I will not make the mistake of saying: "I carried the suitcase." We will praise and honor Him who not only helps us to carry our burdens, but also carries us!

Thank You, Lord Jesus, that Your answer to our sin problem is so wonderful and so clear. Thank You that You said: "Come unto me, all ye who labour and are heavy laden" (Matt. 11:28). Thank You for cleansing us and making us strong. Thank You, Lord. Hallelujah! Amen.

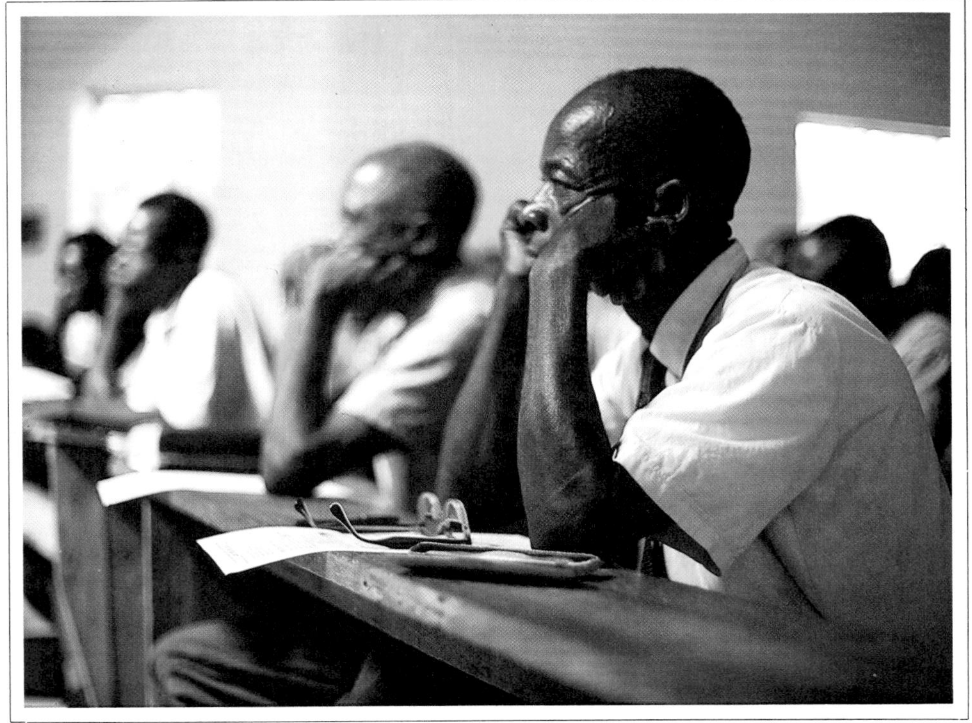

Luampa Mission, Zambia

three

MISSIONARY OR MISSION FIELD

Every human being is either a missionary or a mission field. Have you never opened your heart to the Lord Jesus? Then you are a mission field, and I say to you: Be reconciled to God. Come to Jesus, and take your sins to Him. He died for you on the cross, and He says: "Come unto me, all ye that labour and are heavy laden, and I will give you rest" (Matt. 11:28).

He gives rest and the answer to your problems: redemption, liberation, and life eternal. Then you become a child of God, called to be the light of the world. Therefore, listen to what I am going to say to the missionaries, for you are one of them if you have said yes to Jesus.

A missionary is concerned with the well-being of all those whom he can reach. First Corinthians says: "But the manifestation of the Spirit is given *to every man to profit withal.* For to one is given by the Spirit the word of wisdom; to another the word of knowledge by the same Spirit; to another faith by the same Spirit; to another the gifts of healing by the same Spirit; to another the working of miracles; to another prophecy; to another discerning of spirits; to another divers kinds of tongues . . ." (12:7–10 italics mine).

What riches! Are they meant for you and me? Yes, certainly. Paul says to each of us: "Covet earnestly the best gifts" (1 Cor. 12:31). Yes, this is what a missionary *must* do. How important it is that we reach out

Uganda

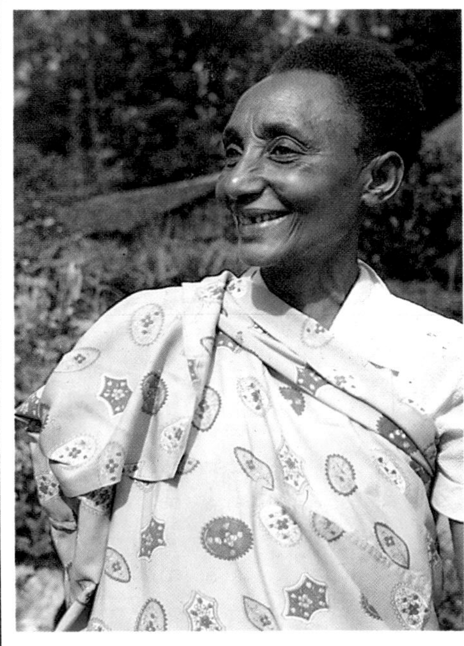

A Ugandan Christian tells of forgiving a person who burned her house.

Russia

for those gifts, as God describes them in His Word through Paul's writings in 1 Corinthians 12 and 14.

Then we shall receive in the things of everyday life, the full meaning of that wonderful Word, that rich promise Jesus gave just before He ascended into heaven: "Ye shall receive power, after that the Holy Ghost is come upon you" (Acts 1:8). The gifts of the Holy Spirit are part of this power. But we must not forget that, between 1 Corinthians 12 and 14, is chapter 13. Paul says here, though we have all gifts and not charity, we have nothing (see 1 Cor. 13:2).

Apart from the gifts there is the fruit of the Spirit: "love, joy, peace, longsuffering, gentleness, goodness, faith, meekness, temperance" (Gal. 5:22–23). And remember, all promises are yes and amen in Jesus. The gifts and the fruit of the Spirit are for you and me. In fact, everything is centered in Romans 5:5: "Because the love of God is shed abroad in our hearts by the Holy Ghost which is given unto us."

When I was in Israel, I noticed much hatred and fear in the hearts of the people. One evening I had spoken about the ocean of God's love, available to us because of the Lord Jesus; and that this love is ready for our use every day, if we make room in our hearts for the Holy Spirit.

After the meeting, a young man came to me and said: "I thank God for what I heard today. The Lord took away all hatred from my heart. Now I can forgive completely. I used to try to, but I could not. Now I have received it by the Holy Spirit."

After a meeting in Berlin one evening, I suddenly recognized a man who came to me as one of the guards at Ravensbrück concentration camp. When I saw this man I remembered all the cruelties he had committed, and I felt bitterness in my heart. But then I felt a wave of love pass through me. That was love through the Holy Spirit.

This man told me: "At Christmas I found the Lord Jesus. I took all my sins to Him. Then I asked for the grace to ask one of my victims for forgiveness. That is the reason I come to you. Will you forgive me all those cruelties?" I could take this man's hand. If we forgive our enemies, we experience the ocean of God's love as never before.

Thank You, Father, in Jesus' name, for the immense riches ready for us, if we accept them by faith. Thank You that all those promises in the Bible are for us. Thank You that then we can also fulfill our missionary calling, not in our own strength, but in Yours. Please, give us many opportunities to do so. Will You open closed doors? Will You take away from us all doubts and all trust in ourselves and instead of these give us faith and trust in You, by Your Holy Spirit? Amen.

Big Sur, California

four

HOW CAN I KNOW WHAT GOD WANTS ME TO DO?

In Isaiah 30:21, we read: "And thine ears shall hear a word behind thee, saying, This is the way, walk ye in it, when ye turn to the right hand, and when ye turn to the left."

Is this really true? Does God lead His children in this way? I want to listen with you to that which the Holy Spirit has to tell us about guidance, for this is sometimes a problem for me, as for many people. There are many who say, "I never hear anything when asking for guidance."

But then my question is, "Do you listen?" Sometimes we have to wait for the Lord, but this waiting can be a blessing in itself, if we do it in the presence of the Lord. Our quiet time is helpful for this.

If you want to hear God's voice clearly and you are uncertain, then remain in His presence until He changes this uncertainty. Often much can happen during this waiting for the Lord. Sometimes He changes pride into humility; doubt into faith and peace; sometimes lust into purity. The Lord can and will do it.

We must also understand that sometimes the silence of the Lord is His way of letting us grow, just as a mother allows her child to fall and get up again when he is learning to walk. If at times God allows a conflict, it may be His way of training us.

Some people say: "But it is very selfish to ask God to give me guidance." Do you know who is telling them that? That is the enemy. The devil is afraid of children of God who safely walk with their hands in the Lord's hand. It is God's will to give us guidance. Let us look at what the Bible has to say about it.

Psalm 32:8 says: "I will instruct thee and teach thee in the way which thou shalt go: I will guide thee with mine eye." Could it be clearer? And Psalm 48:14 says: "For this God is our God for ever and ever: he will be our guide even unto death."

Why is it that so often we do not hear the Lord's voice? I think it is because our sins separate us from Him. The psalmist says: "Mine iniquities have taken hold upon me, so I am not able to look up" (Ps. 40:12).

Satan's work sometimes is like a fog on the outside of the window of our soul, hiding God's light. Sinful desires can cloud the window from the inside. God may put His hand on the window, meaning He is very near. But often disobedience causes us to fail to feel God's guidance or to hear His voice.

When I left the concentration camp during the war, I said: "Now I will travel all over the world, and I shall go wherever God leads me. But I hope that He will never send me to Germany." Because of my experiences in prisons I had a distorted picture of Germany, which was not surprising.

So my obedience was limited: "Everywhere, Lord, but Germany." Then I went to America and when I asked for guidance, I did not receive an answer. That was very hard. Suddenly I asked: "Lord, is there perhaps a sin between You and me?" The answer was very clear: *Germany.* Then I understood and I said: "Lord, then also to Germany."

I went to Germany and found my enemies, but also many friends. In a sense I had more open doors in Germany than anywhere else in the world. And there I experienced that if you love your enemies you touch the ocean of God's love as never before.

So I learned my lesson: Obedience—not "Yes, but," but "Yes, Father."

God guides in a threefold way—first in our prayer time; second by His Word, the Bible; and third, by the circumstances. It is wonderful that in our prayers we not only speak but can also listen. We cannot do so at once; we must get accustomed to it. God's hidden fellowship is found by those who fear Him.

The devil is hindering us from hearing God's voice. That is his goal. There are two rivals of God's voice—our ego and the devil. We must learn to discern who is speaking.

God's commandments are simple, pure, and true. Those of the devil are complicated. He uses doubt, rebellion, and deceit.

It is not at all difficult for the Lord to guide us. And asking things of God gives us a wonderful opportunity to have fellowship with Him. What a comfort it is to know that before we were born, God made His plan for us. He gave us our talents and qualities, and He most certainly will not waste them, now that you are a Christian.

And He, our good shepherd, knows your physical, emotional, and spiritual needs better than you do yourself. He Himself has said: "I will not fail thee, nor forsake thee" (Josh. 1:5). He knows the end from the beginning. He can make every act and experience work together for good for yourself and for others. If only we had a better understanding of what it means to be a child of God.

When you accepted the Lord Jesus as your Savior, He, your Redeemer and Lord, made you a child of God. And if you have not yet accepted Him, I hope that you will do so now.

But we must understand what it means to be a child of God. God is our Father who loves us. We are part of Him. It is not difficult for Him to guide us. He longs to do so, and nothing is too difficult for His omnipotence, and nothing too small for His love. Isn't that wonderful?

O Father, we thank You that we are Your children. And we thank You, Lord Jesus, that You are a good shepherd. Teach us by Your Spirit to clearly hear Your voice. Thank You. Amen.

five

ARE YOU SAFE?

In Colossians 3:3 we read: "Hid with Christ in God." There is no safer place.

Sometimes I show my hands to make this clear. I put the fingers of my left hand over the thumb and then my right hand over my left. You are, I am, the thumb. Jesus is like the fingers covering it; the right hand is God. But to be hidden with Jesus in God is much more wonderful than this illustrates.

Years ago I went to Japan. I did not know anybody or the language, so I felt very insecure, especially when alone. Then I opened my Bible and read:

> Blessed be the God and Father of our Lord Jesus Christ, which according to his abundant mercy hath begotten us again unto a lively hope by the resurrection of Jesus Christ from the dead, to an inheritance incorruptible, and undefiled, and that fadeth not away, reserved in heaven for you, who are kept by the power of God through faith unto salvation ready to be revealed in the last time. Wherein ye greatly rejoice, though now for a season, if need be, ye are in heaviness through manifold temptations: that the trial of your faith, being much more precious than of gold that perisheth, though it be tried with fire, might be found unto praise and honour and glory at the appearing of Jesus Christ: whom having not seen, ye love; in whom, though now ye see him not, yet

New Zealand

India

West German friend

believing, ye rejoice with joy unspeakable and full of glory: receiving the end of your faith, even the salvation of your souls (1 Pet. 1:3–9).

What safety! We are kept for the inheritance; the inheritance is kept for us. I had a glimpse of God's side of the matter.

In Japan everything soon went really well. God opened hearts and doors in a marvelous way for a wonderfully blessed ten months. The bad beginning, however, had been part of the training.

Obedience is very important. Love and obedience belong together. The winds may blow, but there is peace. Jesus was obedient, yes, willing to die on the cross for you and for me. What love!

In the center of a hurricane everything is still. I once experienced this in America, when a storm passed right over our house. A roaring wind blew all around us. Heavy trees were uprooted.

And then suddenly it was quiet; nothing moved. The man sitting next to me said, "Now we are in the center of the hurricane. It is quiet." It was only a moment before the other part of the hurricane passed over us. Real peace only came when the storm had completely passed.

If we are hidden with Jesus in God, the peace remains. "Therefore will not we fear, though the earth be removed, and though the mountains be carried into the midst of the sea" (Ps. 46:2).

Although it may be night, we shall experience: "He that dwelleth in the secret place of the most High shall abide under the shadow of the Almighty" (Ps. 91:1).

Thank You, Lord Jesus, that You give us security in the midst of our insecurities. Thank You that we can be hidden with You in God. Listen, Lord, to those who now surrender to You, trusting You. How wonderful that they are safe in Your arms. Amen.

six

SURRENDER

What is surrender, full surrender? There was a time when this was a great problem for me. Do you also know that feeling? I did not understand what it meant or what to do. Then I read a booklet by Andrew Murray, which really helped me.

First of all I had to understand what *surrender* meant. I read 1 Kings 20:1–4. Benhadad of Syria, with thirty-two allied countries, conquered Samaria, Israel's capital. He sent a message to King Ahab and said: "Thy silver and thy gold is mine: thy wives also and thy children" (v. 3). Ahab answered: "I am thine, and all that I have" (v. 4).

I knew, through experience, such complete surrender. Years ago when I was a prisoner of Adolf Hitler and his followers, I had to surrender my will completely. During the time I was a prisoner, I could not decide anything myself. I just had to obey.

Ahab called Benhadad "My lord, O king" (v. 4), and completely surrendered "all that I have" (v. 4).

But we have to surrender to Someone else, to God, who is love. He is not a dictator; He is a loving Father. There is no limit to what He will do for us, no end to His blessings, if we surrender to Him. Surrender is trusting God. This is altogether different from Ahab's surrender to Benhadad, but it is the surrender God asks from us. He gives a deep rest after we surrender.

When I was a child I loved to sing: "Safe in the arms of Jesus." The

Lord Jesus did not only die on the cross for your and my sins, He lives still and He says: "Lo, I am with you alway, even unto the end of the world" (Matt. 28:20).

Just put your hand into His hand. Then you are safe, even when you cross life's wild torrent of water on a bridge without any rail.

Jesus is Victor, and you can safely surrender to Him.

God expects full surrender from us. Let us for a moment look at all God made. Then we shall see something that can help us to understand this—the sun, the stars, the flowers, the trees are completely in His power.

We ourselves possess things we can only use if we have them completely in our hands. The pen with which I write cannot stay partly in my pocket. Can God use us if He only possesses part of us?

God is life and love and blessing and power and immeasurable beauty, and He is glad to be united with His children, His children who are willing to abide in Him. We, in Him; He, in us.

As you will understand, I am speaking of those who know the Lord Jesus as their Savior and Lord. The first thing that has to happen to us is what Jesus called being "born again." If you know you are a sinner and you ask Jesus to forgive your sins and to come into your heart, He causes the miracle to happen and you are reborn as a child of God. This is very important, but we must not forget that birth is only a beginning. After that we must grow and, time and again, there is the need of a renewed, complete surrender. A lack of complete surrender on our side is a hindrance to God's blessings and use of us, to make us a channel of living water.

Solomon's temple was completely dedicated to God, not just a part of it. Each one of us is a temple of the Holy Spirit; therefore, we must stop compromising, in order that God can do a blessed work through us. It is no longer what *we* can do, but what God can do. Often we will experience that, when we are weak, God is strong.

If you are 100 percent His, you are 100 percent for God's account. An electric subway train is constantly connected with electric current. A bus has to be filled with diesel fuel again and again. If we only give part of ourselves to the Lord in order that He can use us, we are like the bus. The power is continually used up, and we must be filled again. We must be like the electric trains, continually connected with the current. Then we shall go from strength to strength. If we are united with the Lord, we are in His constant care.

O Lord, how much You can do with a man, a woman, who has completely surrendered to You. Thank You that You claim me for the full 100 percent. Will You keep me from dangers and fear and show me the right path, and especially hold me, if I want to take the wrong way? Thank You, Lord. Amen.

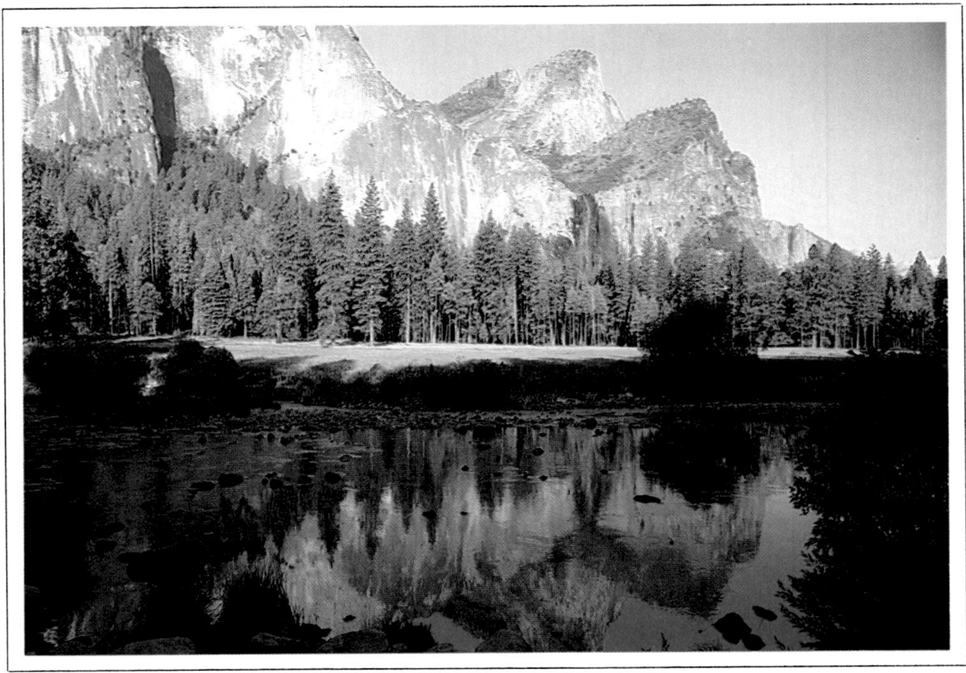

Yosemite National Park, California

seven

THE WORK OF ANGELS

Angels have the gift and the task to praise and thank the Lord. They were present when the earth was created. In the book of Job we can read about their task and discipline; they had to come before God at regular intervals. In Job 38:7 we read about an angels' choir being present at the creation. Best known is their singing in Bethlehem's fields, where one of them brought the message and a multitude sang "Glory to God in the highest, and on earth peace, good will toward men" (Luke 2:14).

Angels are not all-knowing, but they know more than we do. The Bible says that we are a little lower than the angels (see Ps. 8:5). It is evident that they are interested in us because the Lord Jesus says that there is joy in heaven over every sinner who repents (see Luke 15:7), and I am sure that the angels express their joy in singing.

There are ranks among the angels, but we do not know how many. The Bible tells us about two important groups—cherubim and seraphim. When Adam and Eve were driven out of paradise, a cherub stood at the eastern entrance with a fiery sword in his hand to prevent their coming back.

Hezekiah, a man who knew much about God and the things of eternity, walked, if I may put it like this, with the Lord in a childlike way. He took the nasty letter he received from Rab-Shakeh, the Assyrian general during the siege of Jerusalem, to the temple and laid it before the

Lweza, Uganda

Korea

Lord. He then prayed a wonderful prayer that began with these words: "O LORD God of Israel, which dwellest between the cherubims, thou art the God, even thou alone, of all the kingdoms of the earth; thou hast made heaven and earth" (2 Kin. 19:15). In Ezekiel we read about cherubim, and about wheels and wings. One passage describes a tremendous happening in the temple where the cherubim glorified God with a loud voice. It was incomprehensible. The cherubim are described as strange beings, but with hands like those of men (see Ezek. 10:21).

The angels who work on the earth are often described in the Bible as kind, understanding helpers. Read about Peter's liberation in Acts 12:1–11. The Jews so appreciated the murder of James that the king decided to kill Peter, too. He was taken into prison and guarded by a large number of soldiers. He slept with his hands chained to two soldiers. Guards stood at all the doors and in the corridors. After the days of Passover he would be tried. The Christians were together in a twenty-four-hour prayer meeting to entreat God to release Peter.

Then an angel of the Lord came into the cell, and at once there was a light. It seemed that all the guards were asleep. Read what the angel did and how. At first he nudged Peter till he woke up and told him to get up. "Arise up quickly" (v. 7), he said. The chains dropped to the floor. The angel said, in effect, "Get dressed and put on your sandals" and then, "Put on your overcoat and follow me." It is wonderful to read how the angel arranged all the details. At first Peter could not believe all this was real. He thought it was a vision. The angel went before him through open doors, through the gate, and even down the street some distance. Then he disappeared, and Peter found himself all alone on the street in the middle of the night.

In our days the angels are not less active than in those days. In the Congo, missionaries told me of an experience they had. In a home, a kind of boarding school, lived two hundred children of missionaries. Rebels decided to kill all the children and their teachers. Around the house was a low hedge and a few soldiers were in the house, but this was little protection against such a multitude of enemies. When those in the home saw a great number of rebels coming, they all knelt and prayed for protection. Suddenly they saw the rebels turn and run away. The next day the same thing happened, and the third day, again. After this they stayed away.

One of the rebels was injured and was taken to the hospital by people who found him at the roadside. The doctor who was dressing his wounds asked him, "Why did you not enter the house since you intended to kill us?"

The man answered, "We could not. We saw hundreds of soldiers in white uniforms and were terribly frightened."

Now soldiers in Africa never wear white uniforms. Those men had seen angels. The missionaries understood that the angels had protected them.

How great our God is and what a loving Father we have, that He sent those ministering spirits to protect those who will be heirs of salvation!

Thank You, our Father in heaven, that we know that Your angels are here — Your angels who not only were active in biblical days, but who are today surrounding us. Thank You for the great love that is behind this. In Jesus' name, amen.

eight

HOW OFTEN MUST I FORGIVE?

Seventy times seven" (Matt. 18:22).

Come on, how can that be? It will have to be—because you yourself have received forgiveness more than seventy times seven times from Him who warned us: "If ye forgive not men their trespasses, neither will your Father forgive your trespasses" (Matt. 6:15).

And you have prayed: "Forgive us our debts, as we forgive our debtors" (Matt. 6:12).

If you forgive, but do not forget, your heavenly Father will do the same with your sins. It is wonderful that in His Word He uses expressions such as: "As far as the east is from the west, so far hath he removed our transgressions from us" (Ps. 103:12). He causes them to disappear like a cloud. Isn't that great? God throws our sins into the depths of the sea. I like to think that He puts a "No Fishing Allowed" sign there. And this is necessary because the devil loves to fish up forgiven sins; he accuses us day and night.

But how can we learn to forgive like this? A good piece of advice I can give you is this: Immediately forgive the person who says or does anything against you. Then the devil has no chance of letting a shadow remain in your heart.

I believe that Romans 5:5 is the answer: "The love of God is shed abroad in our hearts by the Holy Ghost which is given unto us." Divine love forgives in your and in my heart. Be filled with the Spirit of God and this fruit of the Spirit — love — will be so much stronger than annoyance, indignation, or hatred, that these are changed into forgiving, forgetting, and loving.

I must confess that I thought it was sufficient to forgive. Forgetting I did not take seriously. I had kept letters which recorded nasty things people had done to me, though I had forgiven them long ago. Someone reminded me of what the Lord did with my sins: He forgave and did away with them. Then I burned all those letters in which other people's sins were written, black on white. How happy I was! I experienced that, if the Lord Jesus makes you free, you are free indeed.

In these days we are in training for the kingdom of peace that will come on earth. The Bible is full of promises regarding the things that are going to happen when Jesus returns. Then the wolf will lie with the lamb, swords will be changed into plowshares, nuclear energy will be used to build up, to heal, and no longer to destroy.

Perhaps you say: "Yes, that will be wonderful and then it will be quite easy for me, but now, there is nothing but squabbling, criticism, irritation, especially among Christians. And what morals, what beastliness! Yes, the world lies in evil and the prince of this world is dirty and greedy."

That is true. Especially in this dark world, the Lord Jesus gave us the task of passing on His love. He said, "Ye are the light of the world" (Matt. 5:14), and, "As my Father hath sent me, even so send I you" (John 20:21).

Why did God send His Son Jesus? "To seek and to save that which was lost" (Luke 19:10). Why did Jesus send you and me? To seek that which was lost. And this is possible because, as He said, "Peace I leave with you" (John 14:27), and "Lo, I am with you alway, even unto the end of the world" (Matt. 28:20).

Hand in hand with Jesus, we shall succeed. His love and peace are unending. And however difficult things may be, "We are more than conquerors through him that loved us" (Rom. 8:37).

West Germany

Indonesia

Corrie with friends

United States

African students

Paul was on the front line. You can read it in the book of Acts and in his Epistles. How much adversity and hatred, how much betrayal and slander he had to suffer! And in Romans 8:35 he says, "Who shall separate us from the love of Christ? shall tribulation, or distress, or persecution, or famine, or nakedness, or peril, or sword?"

He could also say, "For thy sake we are killed all the day long; we are accounted as sheep for the slaughter" (Rom. 8:36).

But then he exults: "In all these things we are more than conquerors through him that loved us. For I am persuaded, that neither death, nor life, nor angels, nor principalities, nor powers, nor things present, nor things to come, nor height, nor depth, nor any other creature, shall be able to separate us from the love of God, which is in Christ Jesus our Lord" (Rom. 8:37–39).

Lord, teach me always to forgive everyone, whatever they may do to me, and to burn all the sins of others I have recorded in black and white. Thank You that Your peace in my heart is more than sufficient, yes, that it is overflowing. Hallelujah! Amen.

nine

CITIZENS OF HEAVEN

Philippians 3:20–21 says: "For our conversation is in heaven; from whence also we look for the Saviour, the Lord Jesus Christ: Who shall change our vile body, that it may be fashioned like unto His glorious body, according to the working whereby He is able even to subdue all things unto Himself."

When we were born again, we were born into God's family and the Lord Jesus gave us eternal life — age-abiding life. He made us citizens of heaven.

If we are children of God, we possess this age-abiding life already, whether we are conscious of it or not. My father was very conscious of it. After we had had a joyful evening he often said, "This was a little foretaste of heaven, of the joy we shall have there." But he saw everyday life also in the light of eternity. He said: "My name is on the shop window, but God's name should be there, because I am a watchmaker by the grace of God." I worked with him for twenty-five years and saw that, first, he was a child of God; second, a businessman. He led a sanctified life in home and workshop.

Being citizens of heaven does not make us unworldly, for Psalm 24:1 says, "The earth is the LORD's, and the fulness thereof; the world, and they that dwell therein." If I were a citizen only of this world, I should be in danger of becoming desperate. What do I see all around me? Atheism is gaining ground all over the world; the filthy are getting filthier. The future holds a nuclear war, people say. But the miracle is that we know that the earth is the Lord's. We cannot understand this in the way of logical thinking. It is the foolishness of God that can only be understood by faith.

The Nazi concentration camp was a terrible place. They put the dead bodies into a large washtub. Those who wanted to wash themselves had to step over them. But one day they saw what it meant to be a citizen of heaven — the dead face of Betsie, my sister, was full of heavenly peace and joy, just as the Bible promises.

Jesus once said: "In my Father's house are many mansions. . . . I go to prepare a place for you. And if I go and prepare a place for you, I will come again and receive you unto myself; that where I am, there ye may be also" (John 14:2–3).

Yes, we are expecting the Lord Jesus Christ as Savior, and the signs regarding His return are very clear — it can happen very soon. "Who shall change our vile body, that it may be fashioned like unto His glorious body" (Phil. 3:21).

From what the Bible tells us we know a little about Jesus' glorious body. He could enter a room through closed doors. We read of this when the apostles were together. He ate and drank. He covered large distances. He could make Himself invisible. Read the story about the two who went to Emmaus. But most important of all was the fact that there was no sin, no sickness, no death in Jesus' glorious body.

Our bodies, fashioned like His — the cleansing begins here and now. John speaks about the Lord's return: "Every man that hath this hope in him purifieth himself, even as he is pure" (1 John 3:3). How? Looking at Jesus makes us mirrors of His love. In 2 Corinthians 3:18, Paul says: "But we all, with open face beholding as in a glass the glory of the Lord, are changed into the same image from glory to glory, even as by the Spirit of the Lord."

The words in Philippians 3:20 speak of you and me. Is that really possible? "According to the working whereby he is able even to subdue all things unto himself" (Phil. 3:21). And this power is strong enough to change us — small, insignificant human beings — in such a way that we shall be conformed to Jesus' glorious body. All things He will subdue unto Himself. That is the glorious future. It says in Philippians 2:10 "That at the name of Jesus every knee should bow, of things in heaven, and things in earth, and things under the earth."

Will He then be your Judge or your Savior?

Do you know that you are sanctified, set apart, for such a wonderful reality?

Paul said, "I know whom I have believed, and am persuaded that he is able to keep that which I have committed unto him against that day" (2 Tim. 1:12).

And you and I can say the same.

Thank You, Lord Jesus, that You made us citizens of heaven and that You will change our vile bodies that they may be fashioned like unto Your glorious body. Thank You, Lord, that the best is yet to be. Amen.

ten

MANY RICHES

In Genesis 24:10 we read: "And the servant took ten camels of the camels of his master, and departed; for all the goods of his master were in his hand: and he arose, and went to Mesopotamia."

The servant received an order from his master, Abraham, to look for a wife for Isaac. We also received a command from the Lord Jesus: "Go ye into all the world, and preach the gospel to every creature" (Mark 16:15).

"The gospel" means many riches of our Lord that we have to share. We all have to go where God sends us. Each Christian has a calling: you in your small corner; I, in mine. There is a world to be saved. Do you love the Lord Jesus? Love and obedience belong together.

You have a task—fulfill it! You cannot? Neither can I. We have too little strength and too few riches of our own to share, but our Lord has riches, many, many riches. Therefore, it is necessary that we study our bankbook—the Bible. Withdraw everything you and others need. All God's promises are yes and amen in Jesus. We have to share with many, and therefore, we need the many riches of the Lord.

"Be strong in the Lord, and in the power of his might" (Eph. 6:10). If you know the Lord is your strength, the Lord says, "Go in this your strength." That is what He said to Gideon. A branch of the vine bears

Yosemite National Park, California

fruit if it is connected with the vine. Likewise you and I must remain connected with the Source of strength, our Vine, Jesus.

I hope you who know you are Christians may clearly see how great a task and what great riches you have because you are children of God. But this message is also for you who know you are not children of God. In God's eyes your life is a wilderness, but you can become a garden of the Lord. What can you do? What must you do? Accept Jesus. We read in John 1:12, "As many as received him, to them gave he power to become the sons of God, even to them that believe on his name." And you have work to do, a task to fulfill.

In the Bible we can read of many riches of our Lord. Would you like to follow an intensive course? Then listen to the Master, teaching a very large group of His followers whom He sent out to become the light of the world. You can read all about it in Matthew 5, 6, and 7—the Sermon on the Mount.

But you must not only listen. "Whosoever heareth these sayings of mine, and doeth them, I will liken him unto a wise man, which built his house upon a rock" (Matt. 7:24).

But the intensive course, the Sermon on the Mount, is short. There is a complete manual which we must always study—the Bible. Perhaps you will say, "But I don't understand the Bible." No, we cannot understand it, not from ourselves, but the Lord promised: "Ye shall receive power, after that the Holy Ghost is come upon you" (Acts 1:8).

The Holy Spirit gives you understanding and power and faith. He reveals many riches of our Lord to you. He will show you all you need to become a joyful, victorious child of God. Yes, you will experience what Acts 1:8 also says: "Ye shall be witnesses unto me . . . unto the uttermost part of the earth."

In Ephesians 1:3 Paul says: "Blessed be the God and Father of our Lord Jesus Christ, who hath blessed us with all spiritual blessings in heavenly places in Christ." And this is *now!* These are wonderful riches! *Now!*

According as he hath chosen us in him before the foundation of the world, that we should be holy and without blame before him in love: Having predestinated us unto the adoption of children by Jesus Christ to himself, according to the good pleasure of his will. To the praise of the glory of his grace, wherein he hath made us accepted in the beloved. In whom we have redemption through his blood, the forgiveness of sins, according to the riches of his grace (Eph. 1:4–7).

Just go on reading this first chapter of Ephesians. What a long list of riches! Yes, Jesus is our peace! Ask the Lord to cause your Bible reading by His Holy Spirit to make you see more and more of the great riches of our Lord, which you must distribute to the poor world around you.

Thank You, Lord Jesus, that all Your riches are constantly placed in our hands when we read the Bible. Use us today that we may distribute them. Make us real children of light, the salt of the earth. You caused Abraham's servant to succeed so greatly. Grant us also to experience continuously how wonderful it is to distribute Your riches, our faithful, loving Savior. Hallelujah! Amen.

eleven

SANCTIFICATION

In Uganda there is a greeting: "I owe you nothing; there is nothing between us."

How does it become evident in our lives that we are set apart, that we are sanctified? By our actions and reactions. The above Ugandan greeting is proof that our actions and reactions are right.

Somebody once wrote: "Sanctification means the Holy Spirit, the Holy God in my heart, which makes me conformable to Jesus." I remember that my sister Betsie really grew in sanctification while we were in the concentration camp. The multitude of prisoners in the camp was always a kind of threat. There were so many criminals among them, and everything was dirty. When we passed through a crowd we always had to brush the vermin from our coats. I often was afraid. One day, when quite a crowd came into the barracks, Betsie said: "I love the crowd." Well, this was a reaction of love, a reaction of the Lord Jesus in Betsie. In her own strength she could not have reacted like this.

What happens is that we are being conformed to the image of Jesus. The thought may then enter our minds: *How can this be true of me? How can I have this New Testament experience of sanctification?*

In the first place, complete surrender is necessary. Romans 12:1–2 says: "I beseech you therefore, brethren, by the mercies of God, that ye present your bodies a living sacrifice, holy, acceptable unto God, which

Spain

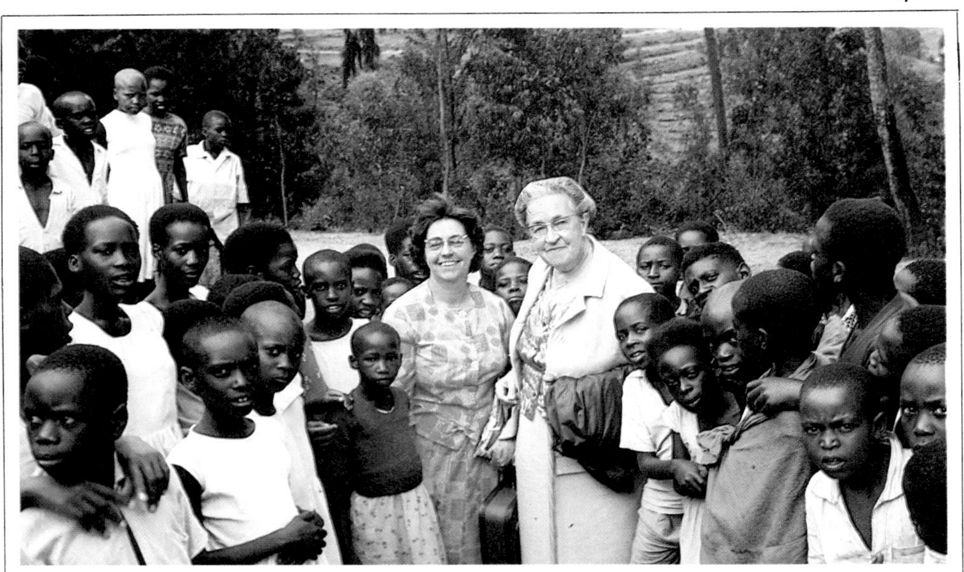

Christians in Rwanda

is your reasonable service. And be not conformed to this world: but be ye transformed by the renewing of your mind, that ye may prove what is that good, and acceptable, and perfect will of God."

A potter can form the clay only if it is completely in his hands. Unconditional surrender is necessary. And if the Lord says to us: "Give Me your heart," and we do it, then we must trust that He will take it. This surrender is not only necessary for the great happenings in our lives, but also in everyday life.

If you have surrendered to the Lord, He is with you and is your guide and your shepherd forever. I mentioned the word *guide.* A mountain climber has a guide with him not only when the path is very steep and full of dangers but also when the path is quite easy and straight. He is with him all the time during an expedition. It is the same with the Lord. He is always with us, today when we are cooking, or writing, or teaching, or doing our office work.

It is quite possible that today there are no difficulties. But the Guide is with us; the Lord is with us. We know He will never leave us if there should be difficulties. I know this from experience.

I accepted the Lord Jesus when I was five years old, and He has never left me alone. There are many battles to be fought before peace will come. But we are not alone in this battle. The Holy Spirit is present, and our secret weapons are our relationship with Jesus and the power of the Holy Spirit. When things are very difficult, we must ask for His help. God sanctifies that which is surrendered to Him. We must surrender. This is a work of grace. God does that which is necessary to mold us. Otherwise nothing will happen. And if we surrender, this is what happens: God cleanses what He takes; He empties what He cleanses; He fills what He empties; and He uses what He fills. This is the showing forth of Jesus Christ, dwelling in us. Surrender never is the end, just as marriage does not end with the ceremony.

Sanctification, however, can bring us into a new conflict, and we have to be careful of that. The devil wants to make us stick to ourselves:

preaching ourselves, looking at ourselves, our faith, our experiences. And then he says, "Just rest on this experience you had."

But this is not right. You must not rest on your experience. It can strengthen your faith, but sanctification is the showing forth of the indwelling Jesus Christ. It is a procedure of daily surrender: a practice in faith, a practice in obedience. A Christian living in the compromise of partial surrender has a really difficult life. Nobody can serve two masters. When you read this now, perhaps you are saying, "Yes, I see. But my faith is not very strong." But you must not look at your faith; you must look at the Lord.

Once I stood before a very primitive bridge in New Zealand. We were not sure if we should cross it in our car. One of the men thoroughly inspected the bridge to see whether it was strong enough. And it was. We safely crossed it. This man did not inspect our faith in the bridge; he inspected the bridge. So often we are inclined to look at our faith, and then we think either that it is strong or that it is weak. But we must not inspect our faith, we must inspect the Bridge. We must not look at ourselves, but at Jesus. And when we look at Him we know that He is strong.

The Holy Spirit will not leave us alone. His peace will reign in our hearts. Sanctification is a decision. The Lord has set us apart for His service. It is an upward-leading path. When climbing a mountain you will not at once be on top; you have to go on and on. But it is wonderful that we are hidden with Christ in God.

Lord Jesus, we praise and thank You that You repair our faith if it does not function well and that You are willing to live in us. We in You, You in us — then we shall overcome like You. How wonderful! We thank You for Your Holy Spirit. Hallelujah!

Bermuda

Russian Christians

twelve

SET APART FOR GOD

"No, you must not use this saucer; it is the cat's." One does not use the cat's saucer oneself. Why? Because it is set apart, not for you, but for the cat.

If we are sanctified, we are set apart by the Lord for His service and for His honor.

I am talking of sanctification because we all know that it is important to be ready for Jesus' return. In the first place, if we are not yet a child of God, we must become one. As soon as we accept Jesus, He gives us the power to become a child of God. This is what He calls being born again. We are born into God's kingdom when we ask the Lord Jesus to come into our lives. But this is only the beginning. After that we must be sanctified. "As obedient children, not fashioning yourselves according to the former lusts in your ignorance: But as he which hath called you is holy, so be ye holy in all manner of conversation; Because it is written, Be ye holy, for I am holy" (1 Pet. 1:14–16).

Sanctification is the continuous working, full of grace, of the Holy Spirit by which He cleanses the sinner and renews his whole nature according to God's image and enables him to do good works. Sanctification has to do with identification. We identify ourselves with the Lord Jesus.

I must say something about the word *identification.* I think of the

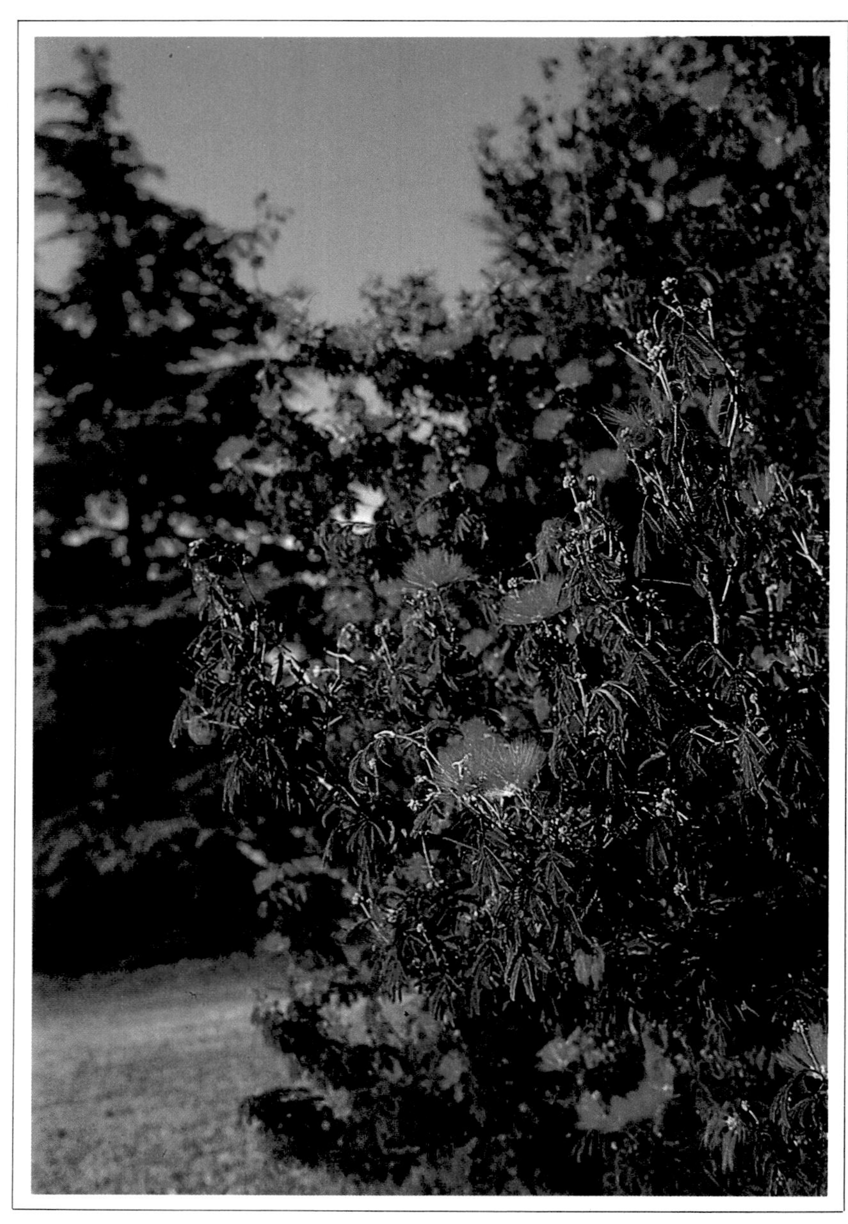

Corrie loved flowering plants of any kind

Japan

Bermuda

time during the war when the Jews had to wear a yellow star. That was a terrible thing, meant to be the beginning of their end. Later on, the Jews were all taken to concentration camps. Father had such great love for the Jews that one day he said, "Sew a yellow star on my coat." He wanted to identify himself with the Jews, even though we knew that then he would not be able to help them. Identification is "becoming alike." The Lord Jesus says: "I am the vine, ye are the branches . . . without me ye can do nothing" (John 15:5).

I think an essential part of sanctification is understanding and accepting that our sins are forgiven. We believe it theologically and theoretically, but it is not always a reality to us.

A little girl once broke her mother's beautiful antique teacup. Very sad about it, she took the pieces to her mother. Her mother said: "I can see that you are sorry. I forgive you. Throw the pieces into the trash bin." The next day the girl saw the pieces there.

She took them out and again went to her mother saying: "Mommy, yesterday I broke this cup." I have an idea that experiencing her mother's forgiveness meant so much to her that she wanted to receive it again.

But her mother said: "Leave those pieces in the trash bin, and only remember my forgiveness."

Do we not often fail to believe in the finished work of forgiveness? Do you ever ask forgiveness for the same sin a second time? Then you are just as silly as that little girl. We must ask forgiveness, believe that we are forgiven, and turn from sin in the strength of the Lord. Turning away from sin is part of sanctification.

You and I must choose for ourselves. Our sanctification is God's will, but, do we love some sin too much to turn away from it? Then we must be careful: "For the wages of sin is death; but the gift of God is eternal life" (Rom. 6:23).

If you accept the Lord Jesus and His forgiveness and His sanctification, it is as if He lifts you out of a vicious cycle and places you in a blessed one. The vicious cycle involves doing wrong things, trying to do your best to stop; succeeding for a while, but stumbling again in weakness. The reason is that the devil is stronger than you are. We all experience this vicious cycle, this battle that makes us desperate.

The Lord Jesus places us in a blessed cycle. Then our battle against sin takes place together with One who is standing on victory ground. You sin even though you are a child of God. But then you repent. When you ask forgiveness, the Lord cleanses you with His blood, and He fills you with the Holy Spirit.

Being filled with the Holy Spirit is just the opposite of sin. Galatians 5:22—23 lists the fruit of the Spirit: "Love, joy, peace, longsuffering, gentleness, goodness, faith, meekness, temperance." This is sanctification—the wonderful sanctification which the Holy Spirit accomplishes in you and me.

Ephesians 6 speaks of the armor of God. This shows us that we do not have victory once and for all; we still need armor. God's armor is strong! If you read correctly you will see that it is the Lord Jesus Himself. He is our Peace; He is our Truth. He, in you; you, in Him. There still will be battles to be fought, but now you are part of a blessed cycle. The devil attacks us. We may fall, but we will rise again. There is forgiveness, cleansing. The path is leading upward and your life will be more and more victorious. The Lord Jesus is going to make you more than conqueror.

Thank You, Lord Jesus, that You take us out of the vicious cycle of sin and falling and place us in the wonderful cycle of forgiveness, redemption, and sanctification. Hallelujah!

thirteen

THERE IS WORK TO BE DONE

The Lord Jesus said: "As my Father hath sent me, even so send I you" (John 20:21).

For what reason did the Father send Jesus? To seek and to save that which was lost. For what reason are we Christians in the world? To seek that which was lost and to bring it to the Lord. This is one of the glorious tasks the Lord gives to us, a task that is for every child of God, for the Lord says: "Ye are the light of the world" (Matt. 5:14), "the salt of the earth" (Matt. 5:13). And in Matthew 28:19 He said we are called to make disciples: "Go . . . and teach all nations, baptizing them in the name of the Father, and of the Son, and of the Holy Ghost."

Are you a Christian, a child of God, to whom the Lord can also say this? If not, then don't wait till the last week of your life, but say today, "Take my life, and let it be dedicated to Your honor, Lord."

If you do this, the Lord will use you to bring the gospel to others. It is wonderful that we have the privilege of doing so, and that we do not need to do it in our own strength. We only have to ask the Lord, and He will do it. He makes us a mirror of His love. A mirror does not do much in itself: It hangs or stands in the right direction, and then it works. You and I need not do much; we only have to look at the Lord Jesus, and He will make us a mirror. And He does it well: He greatly longs for and loves that which is lost. If we let Him speak through us, this love will also come into our hearts. Oh, how wonderful that is!

Each one of us can witness. The Lord wants to use us all to bring others to Him. Sometimes this may be rather difficult, and in these days it can even be very dangerous. In countries without liberty it may be possible that we will have to die for the Lord. In our days there are many martyrs, who, when witnessing for the Lord, are imprisoned or killed.

One day in the concentration camp, I was very encouraged because I was told I was free to go. I stood before the gate and I knew: as soon as this gate opens, I am free. In this concentration camp I had been able to bring the gospel to many women, many had found the Lord Jesus. A great number died with the name of Jesus on their lips. The Lord had used Betsie, my sister, and me to show them the way.

And here I was standing before the gate. My sister had died about two weeks earlier. While I stood there waiting, somebody came to me and said: "Corrie, I must tell you something. Today Mrs. de Boer and Mrs. de Goede both died."

Then I looked at this cruel concentration camp for the last time, and I said: "Thank You, Lord, that You brought me here, even if only for these two women who were saved for eternity, because they found the way to You. You used Betsie and me to that end. Lord, if it were only for these two women, it was worth all our suffering, even Betsie's death."

It is worth living and dying if we are being used to save others for eternity. You and I can be used, whoever we are.

Lord, I thank You — we all thank You — that You want to use us for this great work. Light must be spread, and You want to use us. Thank You, Lord, that You want to use my life perhaps just during the daily routine. Or perhaps You want to send me as an evangelist or a missionary or a pastor, but I thank You, Lord, that wherever we are called, our times are in Your hand. You are the Light of the World, and You make us the light of the world. Hallelujah! Amen.

Friends in England

fourteen
A STEP TOWARD REVIVAL

The evangelist Gypsy Smith was asked one day, "What can I do so that a revival will take place in my church?" The answer was, "Go into your room and take a piece of chalk; draw a circle on the floor and kneel down in the middle of it. Then pray: 'Lord, bring revival to my church, and begin in the middle of this circle.'" That was to the point, wasn't it? But Gypsy Smith was right.

God's will is our sanctification. The Lord Jesus clearly said that we must be born again in order to become a child of God and that we must take our sins to the Lord.

Everybody can become a child of God because that which was done at the cross was complete and for anyone who will believe. All we need to do is to say yes to Jesus from our heart, and then He performs the miracle, making us children of God. This is the beginning. Then we are set apart, in a wonderful way, in Jesus' army. "For wherein shall it be known here that I and thy people have found grace in thy sight? is it not in that thou goest with us? so shall we be separated, I and thy people, from all the people that are upon the face of the earth" (Ex. 33:16).

This is about a sanctified people. A sanctified person has found grace in God's eyes and God goes with him. How great that is! We will not be alone any more, whatever may happen. Therefore we can understand that an unsanctified Christian is out of God's will—a concern for God.

You must understand that you are not responsible for what you are initially but for what you continue to be. Falling into the water does not necessarily mean that you drown, but if you stay underwater you probably will.

Purification, or sanctification, is a matter of serious truths. There is no room for compromise. Somebody once said: "My finger is quite dirty but it *is* pointing to Jesus." This can be the beginning, but it should not remain so. When you point to Jesus and go to Him, He wants to cleanse that dirty finger thoroughly. A pickpocket once said: "I became a Christian. In the past I stole fifty or sixty watches every week, but I don't do that anymore. Now I only steal five or six."

Well, that won't work. Perhaps you shake your head or you laugh at that pickpocket, but are you and I often not just like him? No, we don't steal, we don't deceive—we just dodge taxes a little bit. If you do it cleverly, that is all right, isn't it? No, that is not all right. Nothing like this is all right.

Now, it is possible to live a clean and holy life, *because the Lord is with us*. An unconfessed sin, be it ever so small, a sin of which you did not repent, is very much alive. Please understand that in the Bible we have an answer for our sins and that is a very wonderful thing! So often we think, especially if we are regular churchgoers, that we know what we should do.

I'll never forget a girl in Brazil who told me she was full of doubts: "I once said yes to Jesus, and I thought that then I became a child of God. But I must confess that I no longer believe the Bible. I no longer believe that God exists. In fact, I don't believe anything any more."

Then I read to her from the Bible that the Lord Jesus said that the Holy Spirit will convict us of sin and of righteousness and of judgment. "Of sin, because they believe not on me" (John 16:9). Not to believe in the Lord Jesus is the first sin, a sin bringing forth many more sins. After a while she said: "Oh, I suddenly see it! I have actually committed that sin, the sin of doubting!"

Then I asked her: "Do you know what to do with sin?"

"Yes, of course. I read my Bible."

"Will you do it then? First John 1:9 says: 'If we confess our sins, he is faithful and just to forgive us our sins.'"

"Yes, I will." She folded her hands and said: "Lord, will You help me not to doubt any more?"

But that is not asking forgiveness. That is not the answer to sin! First of all we must ask forgiveness and be cleansed, and then we can ask the Lord to help us. She saw it and humbled herself. She said: "Lord, I committed a great sin. I doubted You and everything the Bible says. Will You forgive me?" As soon as she said this, she was forgiven.

Then I said to her: "Now you can pray that other prayer. First comes confession, then trust that the Lord will put His strong hand on your weak hand."

First Peter 1:17–19 says: "If ye call on the Father, who without respect of persons judgeth according to every man's work, pass the time of your sojourning here in fear: Forasmuch as ye know that ye were not redeemed with corruptible things, as silver and gold, from your vain conversation received by tradition from your fathers; but with the precious blood of Christ, as of a lamb without blemish and without spot."

What a serious matter sanctification is. We were bought with the blood of Christ, a very high price. You, who are a Christian, who act as if you belonged to yourself. . . . Don't forget you lost every right on Golgotha. We were bought lock, stock, and barrel. Jesus paid the price. Did you give the price's value? If you and I do not completely give ourselves to the Lord, we do not give Him the value for which He paid on the cross. The price is high, but it was paid.

Thank You, Lord, that You did this. Will You listen to those who are now saying: 'I know that You have a right to me because You loved me enough to die on the cross for me. I surrender to You completely'? Thank You, Lord Jesus. Amen.

Egypt

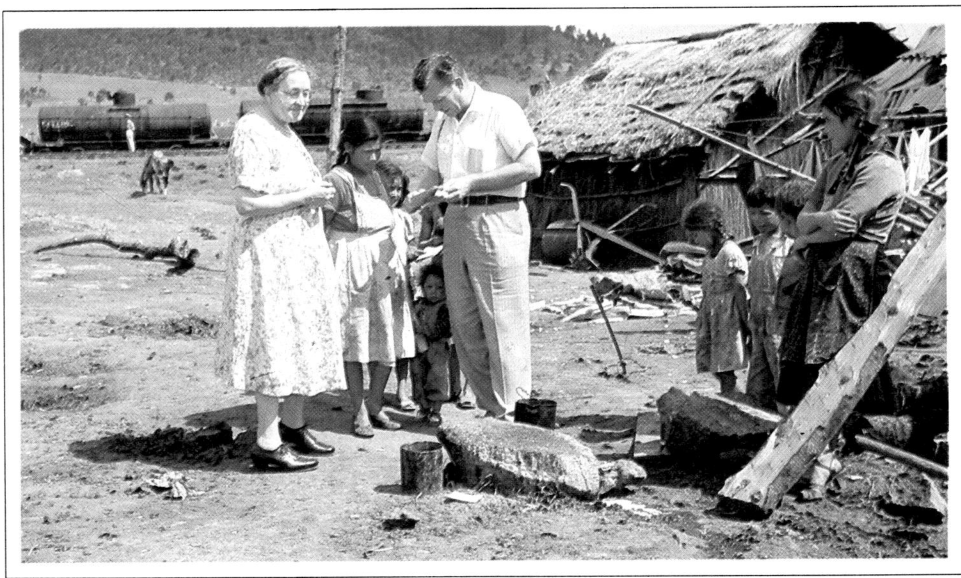

Mexico

fifteen
KEEP WATCH ALWAYS

"Take heed to yourselves, lest at any time your hearts be overcharged with surfeiting, and drunkenness, and cares of this life, and so that day come upon you unawares. For as a snare shall it come on all them that dwell on the face of the whole earth" (Luke 21:34–35).

The cares of this life can keep us so busy that the day of the Lord will come upon us unawares and as a snare. But not only the cares come, but the pleasant things we are looking forward to — the harvest of a new field, a fur coat, a vacation, a Bible study — in themselves such good things.

If at any time our lives were in real danger during World War II during the bombings or while in prison, it was as if suddenly we saw things from God's standpoint. Our perspective was changed because we touched, in a sense, death and therefore eternity. We saw small things, small; great things, great; we saw all things in the right proportion.

Through the conflicts in the Middle East, death touches the world. We do not yet know what it will lead to. Rarely do we read the biblical prophecies together with the newspapers with so much concentration.

The Bible says: "Watch ye therefore, and pray always, that ye may be accounted worthy to escape all these things that shall come to pass, and to stand before the Son of man" (Luke 21:36).

Keep watch always — also today.

It is wonderful that we can be ready—you and I and everyone who belongs to Jesus. It is a matter of complete surrender to Him who said: "Come unto me, . . . and I will give you rest" (Matt. 11:28), and "I am with you alway, even unto the end of the world" (Matt. 28:20).

He loves and longs for you and me. He Himself wants to prepare us for His coming.

First Corinthians 1:8 says: "Who shall also confirm you unto the end, that ye may be blameless in the day of our Lord Jesus Christ." And verse 9: "God is faithful, by whom ye were called unto the fellowship of his Son Jesus Christ our Lord."

And in 1 Thessalonians 3:12–13 we read: "And the Lord make you to increase and abound in love one toward another, and toward all men, even as we do toward you: To the end he may stablish your hearts unblameable in holiness before God, even our Father, at the coming of our Lord Jesus Christ with all his saints."

My father had such wonderful sayings, which he repeated often—but never too often. This is what he said about Jesus:

If He takes us by the hand, He holds us fast.
If He holds us fast, He leads us on.
If He leads us on, one day He will bring us safely home.

Isn't that wonderful? Just put your hand now, at this moment, into His hand.

Thank You, Lord Jesus, that on the cross You bore our sins and those of the whole world, and that You want to make us children of God, everyone who wants to accept it. Thank You that You Yourself want to prepare us for Your coming again by Your Holy Spirit, and that You want us to abound in love one toward another. Thank You that You want to strengthen our hearts. In these turbulent days, we need strong hearts. Thank You that You want to prepare us for that glorious day when we shall see You, face to face. Come quickly, Lord Jesus! Amen.

sixteen

ARE YOU AFRAID OF FULL SURRENDER?

The beginning is what we call conversion, turning toward the Lord Jesus. We have lived so far with our backs toward God. Now we turn 180 degrees toward Him. This is the first glorious step. Then Jesus makes us a child of God.

After that, however, the child must grow, and this means we have to put our weak hands, time and again, into the strong hand of Jesus who wants to go with us and guide us. Your circumstances, your family, your work, your worries, your problems, your suffering, too — if there is suffering — you can give to Him.

There was a time when I was afraid to surrender to Him. "I do not dare," I said. "You never know what consequences it may have. I do not know how to accomplish it, and I lack the courage."

How dreadful to think such things of the Lord, to be afraid of consequences. Then I learned something I want to tell you who are afraid and do not know how to accomplish it: *You do not need to do it in your own strength or by a strong will. God wants to work in you* — both to will and to perform.

In earnest prayer we must find the answer. God who is powerful and full of love wants to work in us Himself, in order to take away all that is wrong, that we may surrender to Him all that is wrong in our thoughts and deeds.

God Himself made Abraham an instrument to His glory.

Then you begin to pray: "God, make me willing to be made willing." I heard this prayer for the first time in New Zealand. A theology student had broken his neck while swimming. He was left paralyzed from neck to toes. He was very intelligent and helped me correct the book I had written in English. One evening we spoke about the fact that he could surrender even the terrible experience he had had. I told him that my sister Betsie, in the concentration camp, had said: "We must not think and speak about our lives in days past, or about what we shall experience when we are free again. We must completely surrender our being prisoners to the Lord. Then we shall be able to accept it."

In the following night I heard the young man pray: "Lord, make me willing to be made willing to surrender all, my life, also my paralysis." The next morning his face was radiant with peace and joy.

If there is something you cannot and dare not surrender, then pray this prayer: "Lord, will You make me willing to be made willing to surrender completely?" If you pray this, your loving Savior is going to do it.

Jesus' life was one of complete surrender. He bought us with a high price. He lives in your heart through His Holy Spirit. You limit Him with your anxiety and unwillingness. He is longing to help you. Trust Him by completely surrendering to Him.

The Germans have a hymn which says: "Instead of thinking of myself, I will throw myself into the ocean of love." This is surrender. There is nothing more glorious—no longer I, but He. As soon as we throw ourselves into the arms of Jesus in full surrender, we shall be surrounded and filled with the ocean of God's love.

It is the Lord Himself who is willing to help us to surrender fully. The Holy Spirit tells us we can go to Him about it. But even when we do so, often doubts enter our hearts: *Was it real? Was it complete?* There is a wonderful verse of Scripture that has greatly helped me. The Lord Jesus said to a father who came to him with his demon-possessed son: "All things are possible to him that believeth" (Mark 9:23). Then this man called out: "Lord, I believe; help thou mine unbelief" (Mark 9:24).

We might say this was faith that had little value, but it did triumph over the devil, and the demon was cast out.

Overleaf: Keto, Yugoslavia

If you and I now come and say: "Lord, I dedicate myself in full surrender to You," this may be said with a trembling heart; we may feel no strength, no certainty at all, but we will succeed. Do not be afraid. Come just as you are, and the power of the Holy Spirit will begin to work in you.

Just now I am reminded of the Lord Jesus in Gethsemane. The Holy Spirit strengthened Him to surrender completely, but what distress, what fear came over Him! If you are weak and fearful, just trust in and surrender to the work of God's Spirit in you. Trust that God accepts you.

Look up to Him. Sometimes we are much occupied with ourselves, but we must be occupied with God. Don't be afraid to say: "Lord, I do not quite understand, but I accept Your conditions that I must and can surrender completely so that You will bless me and make me a blessing." If you say this in your heart—perhaps with fear and trembling—then you can be assured that God will take notice of it. He listens, He writes it into His Book, and from that moment, He takes complete possession of you. Perhaps you do not feel it, or realize it, but now you belong completely to Him.

It is such joy that we can talk about all things with Him. Just tell Him everything—you have doubts, you do not understand, or whatever it may be. You belong to Him. And now you must not only talk to Him, but also listen to His voice.

There is an old story about a lost brooch that greatly helped me. A valuable brooch was lost in a theater. The owner noticed this loss only when she came home. Early the next morning she called the hall porter of the theater and asked him whether he had found a brooch.

"No," the man said, "but where did you sit? I shall go and look. Perhaps it is under your seat."

"I was in the second seat on the fifth row."

The man went and looked and found the brooch. He returned to the telephone and said: "Yes, I am so glad. I found your brooch! Hello? Hello?" There was no answer. The lady had put down the receiver and never knew that her brooch had been found.

The Holy Spirit teaches us to expect much of the Lord.

Listen to the Lord. If you do not hear His voice at once, then wait patiently. He is a Good Shepherd, and a good shepherd talks to his sheep. Waiting on the Lord is a blessing in itself. Do not immediately put down the receiver. He loves you, and He longs to say many things to you!

Lord Jesus, thank You that we no longer need to try and try, because You want to work in us by Your Holy Spirit. Thank You for loving us so much. Please, forgive us that often we have little time and patience to listen to You. Thank You that You are willing to do everything we cannot do. Show us how we can completely surrender and why we must do so. Thank You for accepting us when we surrender. Hallelujah!

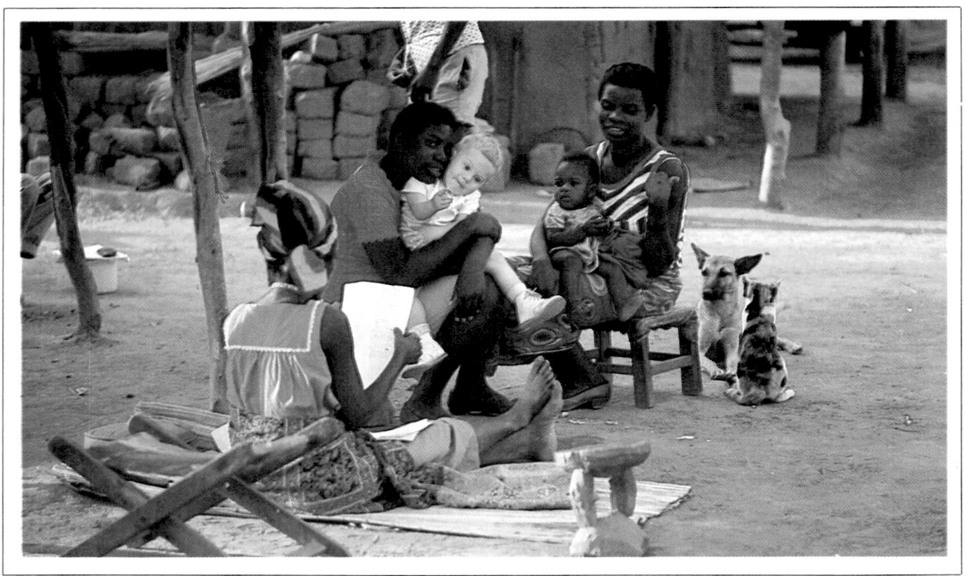

Joseph's Village, Zambia

seventeen

BLESSED SLEEP

Did you sleep well last night?

The Bible says that God gives sleep to His beloved children. I experienced this when I was a prisoner in Ravensbrück. What a blessing it was to sleep! That was the only time we could forget our misery; awakening was hard because then we had to accept the terrible reality of being prisoners again.

When I was in solitary confinement, morning was the worst time of the day. I soon learned to sing, as soon as I woke up: "Stand up, stand up for Jesus!" This gave me new courage to face each day. And one morning, I heard someone in another cell answer in song, as if to say, "I know this Jesus, too!" That was a wonderful blessing.

One person in the Bible who seemed to sleep at the strangest times was Peter. The first time was on the Mount of Transfiguration. Can you imagine going to sleep when such wonderful things were happening? One might call this the sleep of immaturity. When he awoke, his reaction was wrong also. He at once wanted to build a tabernacle for Jesus, for Moses, and for Elijah, as if they were all on the same level. But Peter's plans came to nothing.

Later Peter slept in the Garden of Gethsemane when Jesus greatly needed him. Even when the Lord reprimanded him, Peter slept on. This was a sleep of disloyalty.

These examples show how Satan can use sleep to defeat us. What were your last thoughts before you went to sleep last night? I have learned that when I fall asleep while reading the Bible or praying, a wonderful fellowship with the Lord continues, even in my dreams.

Dreams can be a strategic point for the Enemy since we cannot control them. Before I go to sleep, I often pray, "Lord, will You fill my subconscious with Your peace and love, by Your Holy Spirit?" The Lord always gives His peaceful sleep, far more wonderful than that given by sleeping pills.

I also had to ask Him for help when I traveled a great deal, because I had difficulties with the differences in time, atmosphere, and climate after long airplane trips. It usually took two days for my old body to adjust.

I once traveled to Uzhikistan, in the Soviet Union near Siberia, to speak at several meetings. There was a five-hour time difference from Holland, and when I arrived I told my hosts that I would not be able to speak until the following day.

"But two meetings have already been arranged," they replied.

"All right," I agreed, "but I must rest between meetings."

After the first meeting they took me to a home where they had a lovely bed with many pillows and a lace bedspread over them. I slept wonderfully.

After the second meeting they took me to another home to sleep. In the bedroom were two beds. In one of them was an old lady. I discovered that she spoke German, and I had the joy that the Lord used me to cause her to accept Him. That was a blessed sleep!

Lord, thank You for giving us rest so that we may serve You when we are awake. We entrust our sleep time to You and ask that You protect us from the evil one. And when Your work means sacrificing sleep, help us remember that You are our strength. In Jesus' name, Amen.

eighteen

HOW DO PEOPLE BECOME OPPRESSED OR POSSESSED BY DEMONS?

Often we can find the reason for demon possession in occult sins. This is very evident in the case of fortunetelling. In Deuteronomy 18:10–13 we read:

> There shall not be found among you any one that maketh his son or his daughter to pass through the fire, or that useth divination, or an observer of times, or an enchanter, or a witch, or a charmer, or a consulter with familiar spirits, or a wizard, or a necromancer. For all that do these things are an abomination unto the LORD: and because of these abominations the LORD thy God doth drive them out from before thee. Thou shalt be perfect with the LORD thy God.

When I worked in Germany after the war, people often came to me saying they could not pray. They could not concentrate when reading the Bible or when listening to a sermon. Often they were tortured by thoughts of suicide, an especially clear indication of the influence of demons. Later I found out what the cause of this was.

Shortly after the war, many men and boys were missing in Germany. Their relatives did not know whether they still were in concentration camps in Russia or whether they had died. This uncertainty was terrible. Some of these people went to fortunetellers. I don't know whether they received any appropriate information, but this was the cause of the darkness I met later on when counseling. Because of this sin, the door had been opened to an evil power. Often it was not difficult to convince people that this was a sin in the eyes of the Lord. In Deuteronomy 18:12 the Bible very clearly states: "All that do these things are an abomination unto the LORD." Going to fortunetellers shows that a person looks for help with the Enemy instead of trusting God's power.

It was wonderful to explain how they could be set free. Read 1 John 1:7 and 9. After realizing they had sinned, they could take this sin to the Lord, confess it, and ask forgiveness for it. Then this promise became a reality. The Lord forgave and cleansed them with His blood. A heart He has cleansed with His blood, He wants to fill with His Holy Spirit. The fruit of the Spirit is, among other things, peace and joy.

Not only does fortunetelling open the door for the powers of darkness, but so also does participating in spiritualistic experiments. Very often when I warned against fortunetelling and spiritualism or asked people whether they had ever participated, they replied, "I just did it for fun" or "I did not believe in it."

Then I used this example: In Germany there now is a wall through Berlin. Formerly this wall was not there, but half of the city was forbidden territory for the inhabitants of West Berlin. At some places the boundary line went through a wooded area. Imagine a person playing in such a woods and accidentally getting into East German territory. Then he would be arrested, and it would not help him to say: "I just did it for fun." If one is on the Enemy's territory, one is in his power. It is the same with sins of witchcraft one commits for fun.

Another very dangerous sin is wearing amulets. We cannot be too strict about this. Once I heard of a girl who was always ill. Somebody gave her an amulet she was to wear around her neck. The illness was cured immediately, but the child was very gloomy; she never smiled, and when she was twelve years old she tried to commit suicide. An evangelist visited her and asked her whether she had an amulet. She gave it to him but begged him not to open it.

He opened it all the same and found a piece of paper in it. On it was written: "I command you, Satan, to keep this body healthy until you have this soul in hell." The amulet was destroyed, and the child was set free; but she fell seriously ill again at once. Afterwards she was healed by the laying on of hands in the name of Jesus.

Apart from fortunetelling and wearing amulets and charms, the cause of being in darkness can also come through contact with false doctrines or people practicing demonic influence, such as palmists and magicians. Reading horoscopes and being occupied with the sins of others and with people who are demon-possessed can also bring us into contact with evil powers.

It is not without reason that Paul warns Timothy not to lay hands on anybody too soon. Hypnotism is also a danger. The Bible very clearly points out that it is sin to get into touch with those who have died. Reading wrong books also can bring us into great darkness. All books on witchcraft and amulets should be destroyed.

In Indonesia during a great revival, again and again, those who surrendered to the Lord repented of their sins and burned and destroyed all items of witchcraft—idols, amulets, and occult books. Because we live in such a grave time, every compromise is an especially great danger. If we choose to be on Jesus' side, we are the children of light in the midst of a dark generation. But our choice must be very definite. What joy that with Jesus there is forgiveness and redemption!

Dear Father, in Jesus' name we pray that You will show us very clearly whether there is still any compromise in our lives, in our hearts, with Satan and his demons. Thank You that You want to set us free and that You will cleanse us by the blood of Jesus, Your dear Son. Strengthen us by Your Holy Spirit. Amen.

nineteen

ARE WE POWERLESS AGAINST DEMONS?

The book that can give us the most practical knowledge of demons is the Bible. At the same time it is the book in which we are taught victory over demons. In these days in which there is such a big mobilization of evil powers all over the world, it is practical and necessary to know how a child of God, a Christian, should stand against these powers. We very definitely read that there are two strong weapons available — the blood of Jesus Christ and the authority of His name.

What does "the blood of Jesus Christ" mean? It points to the finished work on the cross. When Jesus gave His blood in order to save us from sin — and not only us, but the whole world — He bought us when He died that terrible death and said: "It is finished!" (John 19:30).

However, it means more. "If we walk in the light, as He is in the light, we have fellowship one with another, and the blood of Jesus Christ his Son cleanseth us from all sin" (1 John 1:7).

That means *now.* We know that Jesus did not only die for us, but that He lives and He still wants to cleanse our hearts with His blood, if we confess our sins to Him.

The devil is afraid of the blood of Jesus and even of His Word. That is not surprising! In the book of Revelation it says: "They overcame him by the blood of the Lamb" (12:11).

We should never speak to people who are under the direct influence of the devil without first of all asking for the protection and the cover of Jesus' blood. We overcome by the blood of the Lamb.

Although we may not understand this, we shall experience that God is serious about His promises, if we act in obedience to His Word. The foolishness of God is so much wiser than the wisdom of the wise (see 1 Cor. 1:25). Only knowledge because of faith can comprehend these things.

We also must remember that the normal and safe position for every believer is to be "crucified with [Christ]" (Rom. 6:6).

If, in the collision with satanic powers, the children of God appeal to the protection of Jesus' blood on "uncrucified" flesh, they remain open to the influence of Satan's spirits. Speaking about the cleansing and keeping power of the blood and, at the same time, not understanding that being crucified with Christ is inseparably connected with it, means the full redemptive power of Golgotha is misunderstood.

The second strong weapon we have in our hands is the wonderful name of Jesus. Jesus told us what we can and must do in His name. "In my name shall they cast out devils" (Mark 16:17). In the name of *Jesus,* not *Christ. Christ* is His title. But the name that is above every name is *Jesus.*

The third great source of power we have in the promise of Acts 1:8: "Ye shall receive power, after that the Holy Ghost is come upon you." Then the Lord gave us the big task to go into the whole world and make all people His disciples: "And ye shall be witnesses unto me both in Jerusalem, and in all Judaea, and in Samaria, and unto the uttermost part of the earth." But before He gave this big commandment, He said: "Ye shall receive power, after that the Holy Ghost is come upon you."

The gifts and the fruit of the Spirit make us strong in the battle against evil powers. So if we ask ourselves if we are powerless against demons, we can reply with a strong no. Jesus Christ's victory is *our* victory. On our side are a mighty High Priest and legions of angels. They that are with us are much stronger than they that are against us.

It is necessary to recognize the Enemy before being able to conquer him. We must be careful about the following, equally bad, though opposite, errors, which our generation can make concerning demons. One is to believe they do not exist. The other one is to believe they exist and to have an unhealthy interest in them.

In his book *The Screwtape Letters,* C. S. Lewis has a demon write to his nephew who is in the world in order to lead men astray. He says: "At first you must try to let them believe we do not exist. If they know we do exist, then you must cause them to think and talk about us as much as possible."

Let us not forget that God wants and expects us to be conquerors over the powers of darkness, not only because of our personal victory or the setting free of others from the bondage of Satan — although these things are very important — but to the glory of God, in order that His triumphs over His enemies may be made manifest. It is important that we should take the right position. The Bible tells us: that we must be *in* Christ, "above all principality, and power, and might, and dominion" (Eph. 1:21); that we are called to "resist the devil" (James 4:7); that we must "put on the whole armour of God" (Eph. 6:11); that we must resist the devil in the power of Jesus' blood, by faith, prayer, and sometimes fasting.

Jesus cast out demons, and He commands His disciples to do the same. That is what He expects from us. In the book of Acts we read how the disciples used the authority given to them by casting out demons. In this way they glorified the name of Jesus.

We must never forget that God's Word holds good forever and that His commandments mean to us exactly the same now as they did two thousand years ago for the disciples. Those who act according to them in obedience shall receive God's almighty power in the same way. Be strong, not in yourself, but in God, in the power of His limitless majesty. Put on the whole armor in order that you may be able to withstand all satanic methods of attack. Because (as I presume you will have understood by now) our battle is not against some physical enemy, but against spiritual powers ruling this dark world, and against the messengers of the devil's headquarters itself. For this you need the whole armor in order to be able to withstand in the evil day, and having done all, to stand.

Jesus *was* victor, Jesus *is* victor, and *Jesus shall be victor!*

Thank You, Lord Jesus, that we do not need to fear, although the powers of the Enemy are strong and manifold. Will You open our eyes that we may see what great task we have in this dark world, and how we can conquer? Forgive us when we live as weaklings, when we can be strong and rich because of Your many promises that are true. Thank You that You Yourself will make us strong in You. Hallelujah. Amen.

Capernway Hall, United States

twenty

CANNOT MUST BECOME *CAN*

John 7:37–39 says: "In the last day, that great day of the feast, Jesus stood and cried, saying, If any man thirst, let him come unto me, and drink. He that believeth on me, as the scripture hath said, out of his belly shall flow rivers of living water. (But this spake he of the Spirit, which they that believe on him should receive . . .)."

Jesus called: "Come!" He did not say it softly so that only people standing near Him could hear. He called out loudly so that all heard it. And He also says to you: "Come!"

Perhaps you will say: "Oh, that may be for that other person, for my decent neighbor who goes to church regularly and who is good, but it is not for me. I am much too sinful; I would not dare. Oh, no, I cannot become religious; I am far too bad for that."

Well, if this is what you say, it is just what is needed. There is only one kind of person whom the Lord Jesus did not accept. When He said: "Come!" and they answered: "Yes, here I am, Jesus; I am good" (some of these are called Pharisees), then the Lord Jesus said: "Are you so good? Then I am sorry, but I cannot help you." But if such a Pharisee said: "In the eyes of men I am very good, but there is sin in my heart," then the Lord Jesus said: "Just come to Me, and I shall help you."

If you say: "I am too bad to come to Jesus," then you are just the person He wants to help. So come. Jesus loves *sinners*. He loves only sinners. He has never sent away sinners who asked forgiveness for their sins. He died on the cross for sinners. Only for sinners He suffered awfully on the cross, so awfully that He said: "My God, my God, why hast thou forsaken me?" (Mark 15:34).

All this He did for sinners like you, so come! And when you come to Him, He will set you free from your sins. You must confess them; take them to Him. If you look at Jesus in His great love, if you see Him in faith, then you feel ashamed of yourself. Then you will pray: "O Lord, be merciful unto me, a sinner."

And do you know what is wonderful? That He is merciful to sinners. Now you can take your sin to Him. You can say: "Lord, this is wrong, and this is crooked, and that is miserable, and I said this, and I thought that." If you confess this, it will be as if a load is taken away from you. If you come to Jesus, the burden of sin drops from your shoulders. And if you have confessed your sins, you must turn away from them completely. John says: "If we confess our sins, he is faithful and just to forgive us our sins, and to cleanse us from all unrighteousness" (1 John 1:9).

Then you have not only confessed your sins, but the great miracle takes place that Jesus cleanses you with His blood. What is the blood of Jesus? I don't understand how it works; but I do know what it means. Jesus gave His blood on the cross to redeem you and me — a tremendous price. When you speak of the blood of Jesus, you think of the finished work on the cross.

But do you know that if you take your sin to Jesus, He forgives you and throws your sin into the depth of the sea? That is what the Bible says. The devil would love to make things hard for you because of those sins that have been confessed. But the sins that have been taken to the Lord are dead. The Bible says that He has removed our transgressions from us as far as the east is from the west. He causes them to disappear as a cloud that vanishes. When a cloud vanishes, it never comes back.

And then the Lord puts His Spirit into your heart, with the fruit of the Spirit — just the opposite of your sin — love, joy, goodness, purity.

Will there not be any more temptations? Oh, yes, the devil is not likely to leave you in peace. But I can advise you to take the sin immediately to the Lord. This is necessary because otherwise the devil accuses you. He accuses God's children day and night, the Bible says. But if you have taken it to the Lord, even if it is only two minutes before the devil comes to accuse you, then you have nothing to fear. Then the Lord will cast this sin into the depths of the sea, and it will be gone. The devil has nothing more to say.

Thank You, Lord Jesus, that You came to save sinners, to make them happy, to set them free, to give them peace instead of discord. Thank You that he or she who for the first time today understood that he or she can come may know that Your hand is stretched out toward him, toward her; and that You are saying: "Come!"

Lord, did You see? Of course You saw! You heard when they said: "Yes, I come, Lord Jesus." Oh, how wonderful, Lord! You are going to do that marvelous thing in their lives, that they will be strong in the battle, that You will fill them with Your Holy Spirit. Thank You, Lord Jesus! You make sinners happy—especially sinners—and You set them free. Hallelujah! What a Savior You are! Amen.

twenty-one

GOD'S FOOLISHNESS IS HIGHER THAN OUR WISDOM

Many years ago I worked in Haarlem [in the Netherlands] among mentally retarded people. I had several Bible study clubs with them. It was a great work.

You and I need the Holy Spirit to understand eternal truths. The foolishness of God is the greatest wisdom. We cannot understand it with worldly wisdom.

In 1 Corinthians 1 and 2 we can read about this. I always see that there are two levels: the wisdom of the wise, which God gives to us as a privilege, and then a little higher the foolishness of God. We can only understand this through the Holy Spirit as the highest wisdom.

We should never try to bring the foolishness of God down to the level of the wisdom of the wise and, by doing so, try to understand it. Then we come to the strangest conclusions. Some think that God is dead. They got this idea because they acted in the way I mentioned just now. They made logical thinking their guide.

Brother Andrew once said: "What, is God dead? Oh, no, I talked to Him this morning." In his quiet time he experienced the foolishness of God. God, who made heaven and earth, talked with him, a small human being. Never pull down the foolishness — the highest wisdom — of God and judge it with the wisdom of the wise. If we want to see reality, we must lift up the wisdom of the wise to the level of the foolishness of God.

Then we shall see and understand.

The mentally retarded people had very little wisdom of the wise. But the Holy Spirit gave them a great deal of the foolishness of God, which they accepted much more easily and without doubts. They also understood it. Then I saw the truth of the Word that we must become like children, so that we can enter the kingdom of heaven. I could never tell them too much of God's love. Then their faces were radiant.

The father of one of the retarded girls once asked me: "Why is my daughter not allowed to take part in the Lord's Supper? She loves the Lord. Does it really matter that she cannot learn?" My answer was: "Pray about it this week. I shall also do so."

I did, but I also went to a pastor with whom I discussed the possibility that she be baptized and confirmed and take part in the Lord's Supper.

All this was about fifty years ago. There were no organized ministries to the retarded at that time. Nowadays it is much better and easier. This pastor and I prayed together. And it became possible. The only thing he said was, "But you must explain it to them; I cannot do it simply enough."

Then I translated the whole printed order of the Lord's Supper, making a story out of it. I remember the words: "They that eat and drink unworthily, eat and drink a judgment on themselves."

"Once there was a lady," I began, "who did not at all believe that the Lord Jesus died on the cross for her. She never asked Him to forgive her sins. And do you know what she did? She took part in the Lord's Supper, took the bread and the wine which are signs of the Lord's body and blood, through which we receive forgiveness."

The reaction was that the whole class said: "Oh, how terrible!"

I said: "Yes, how terrible. And do you know who said so, too? The Lord Jesus."

I have never so much enjoyed a Lord's Supper as that time together with this class. There was an understanding, a thankfulness, an earnestness over which the angels must have rejoiced.

And then the baptismal service! Jack, a big fellow with no more understanding than a six-year-old, knelt down and heard those wonderful words from the pastor's lips: "Jack, I baptize you in the name of the Father, and of the Son, and of the Holy Spirit." He felt the water on his forehead. And Jack was enjoying it so much that he wanted to hold it fast. He did not rise, but remained kneeling on the floor. I took his hand and brought him back to his seat. But Jack kept his eyes tightly shut. He wanted to hold it fast. It was very touching.

Thank You, Lord, that You give salvation to children, to mentally retarded people, and that You give it to those who read this now. Thank You, Lord Jesus, that You said: "Come unto me, all ye that labour and are heavy laden, and I will give you rest" (Matt. 11:28). How much You love us, Lord! Amen.

Korea

A friend in Argentina

Cocos Islands

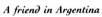

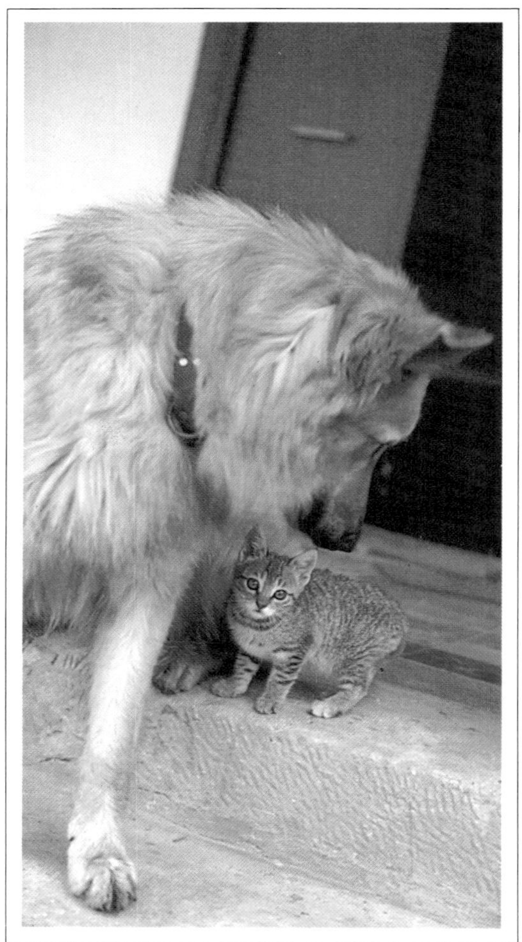

Animal friends in Lweza, Uganda

Witnessing to U.S. servicemen and women

A New Zealand associate

twenty-two

NOT FEAR, BUT LOVE

"God is our refuge and strength, a very present help in trouble. Therefore will not we fear, though the earth be removed, and though the mountains be carried into the midst of the sea" (Ps. 46:1–2).

"Men's hearts failing them for fear, and for looking after those things which are coming on the earth" (Luke 21:26).

One of the signs of the times that we can expect Jesus' return soon is the fear in the hearts of men. When the securities, the certainties of our lives are shaking as never before, there is good reason for fear. Property is insecure; a good position in life, a large bank account do not give security.

Now that many children of God begin to see the signs of the times and read the book of Revelation as something that is possible this year (and has already begun perhaps), there is a sort of awakening. In America many Christians are occupied with the near future, when we shall not be able to buy or sell, if we refuse the mark of Antichrist (see Rev. 13:17). Now they are seeking refuge in houses and farms with land to grow food. Is that necessary? I do not know.

I believe that God's children will experience great miracles of protection and deliverance, even if they pass through tribulation. The Bible gives many securities for now and for what is coming. "For God hath not given us the spirit of fear; but of power, and of love, and of a sound mind" (2 Tim. 1:7).

It is very important to make room in our hearts for the Holy Spirit; then we shall not fear, though the earth be removed. When the situation is very dangerous we no longer can count on our own strength. That is a blessing. In countries where Christians suffer great tribulation, even persecution, I have seen how the Lord used weak people and children as channels of streams of living water. Their own strength was not enough, but they trusted Him who filled them with the Spirit — not of fear, "but of power, and of love, and of a sound mind." They saw the dangers but also the reality of Jesus' victory.

When I was in a concentration camp I did not know that I would be one of the 20 percent of women who left it alive. I looked death in the eyes. When we touch eternity we see all things so simply. It was as if I saw the devil who was much stronger than I. But then I saw Jesus, who is much stronger than the devil, and together with Him I am much stronger than the devil. Then fear has to leave.

Those who are with us are more and stronger than those who are against us. "Greater is he that is in you, than he that is in the world" (1 John 4:4). What we can expect, and already begin to see, is that apart from fear there will also be much hatred. Romans 5:5 is wonderful. The Holy Spirit in our hearts — this means that the Lord Jesus gives God's love into our hearts by the Holy Spirit who is given to us. That love is an immovable thing in the coming days.

Human love fails and will always fail. God's love never fails and we shall experience this, we and those with whom we get into touch, for they will see in us that there is no fear, but victorious love, the love of God. "There is no fear in love" (1 John 4:18).

There will no longer be room for compromise. It will be yes or no. Extremes — hatred or love — will govern. Religion is no security. Antichrist will be very religious, and he will even make up a world religion, in which he himself will be god. World history is confused and will grow more so.

Like being in a dangerous thick fog, man will live without perspective. The Holy Spirit will clearly show us God's perspective. Already we can see God's plan. The things we experience now are signs of the times, clearly foretold in the Bible, and pointing to the great solution, the wonderful future of God's kingdom, that will come on earth. "For the earth shall be filled with the knowledge of the glory of the LORD, as the waters cover the sea" (Hab. 2:14).

Then the leaves of the tree of life will be for the healing of the nations (see Rev. 22:2). So there is a future for the nations.

The future is glorious. The best is yet to be, and you and I have the privilege to help hasten the coming of Jesus. Be filled with God's Spirit, then there will be no fear, but the love of God that conquers.

Thank You, Lord Jesus, that You send God's love into our hearts by the Holy Spirit who is given to us. Thank You that this love will win and that it remains and will cause us not to fear; though the earth be removed and the mountains be carried into the midst of the sea. Hallelujah! Come quickly, Lord; yes, come quickly. It is dark on earth. Prepare us for the great feast. Thank You, Lord. Amen.

twenty-three

PRAY FOR ONE ANOTHER

When Paul is writing about the armor of God which we need in order to be strong in the Lord and in the power of His might, he says in Ephesians 6:18–20: "Praying always with all prayer and supplication in the Spirit, and watching thereunto with all perseverance and supplication for all saints; and for me, that utterance may be given unto me, that I may open my mouth boldly, to make known the mystery of the gospel, for which I am an ambassador in bonds."

There are many ambassadors for Christ who need these prayers right now. A missionary was in great danger and one evening, was alone in his house. Enemies wanted to kill him, but nothing happened. The next day one of these came to him and said: "Last night we intended to kill you, but we could not."

"Why not?"

"There were too many men around your house. There were only four of us and about seventeen men stood around your house."

The missionary wrote this to his friends at home. They came to the conclusion that on this particular night they had had a prayer meeting—seventeen had come to pray.

Seventeen believers prayed at home.

Seventeen angels stood around the missionary's house.

Satan laughs when we exert ourselves. He sneers at our wisdom. He trembles when we pray.

Yosemite National Park, California

When you pray for others, it is as if you went and stood beside the Lord and together you talked about their needs.

There are some who say you must have compassion on others in a humanistic way. But I believe we should be careful with this. I do not believe it is right to try to identify with a person who is in danger of perishing in need or in sin. This can infect and break us. And it is not necessary. God does not ask this of us.

Jesus bore all our griefs and sins on the cross, and He finished the work of salvation. Is there anyone else as able to understand our griefs as He who bore everything on the cross?

Is there anyone who can fathom the dangers of sin better than He who paid for these sins with His blood and so great a love, the ocean of God's love?

Therefore, together with Him, we can understand sorrows and see sins in their true color. The chastisement of our peace was upon Him. With His stripes we are healed.

Then intercession does not become the patching up of a person's soul, but the soul's breaking through to contact with God. We can only really intercede if we pray with the reality of God's redemption in Jesus Christ as a starting point.

As an intercessor in God's kingdom you must be careful to keep in pace with the reality which God is showing you, for otherwise you can well be overrun. If you know too much, more than God gives you to know, the situation will so terribly oppress you that you cannot penetrate to the reality of the situation.

Intercession is very important.

A little girl prayed for her friend till she also found the Lord Jesus as her Savior. Together they began to pray for a third girl. Then the three of them for a fourth and the four of them for a fifth — the chain reaction in the hearts of little children by intercession.

Will you not ask the Lord to use you for this chain reaction — that this may begin in your heart and then continue? Pray for one, then together for a third, then the three of you for a fourth.

In 1 Timothy 2:1–2 Paul says: "I exhort therefore, that, first of all, supplications, prayers, intercessions, and giving of thanks, be made for all men; for kings, and for all that are in authority; that we may lead a quiet and peaceable life in all godliness and honesty."

I have experienced that nothing makes us as free as interceding for others.

What a heavy task! But how glorious!

Lord Jesus, will You make us real intercessors? We dare to be such, together with You, and we praise and thank You that Your redemption on the cross is a greater reality than all the pains and sins of those around us. Hallelujah! Amen.

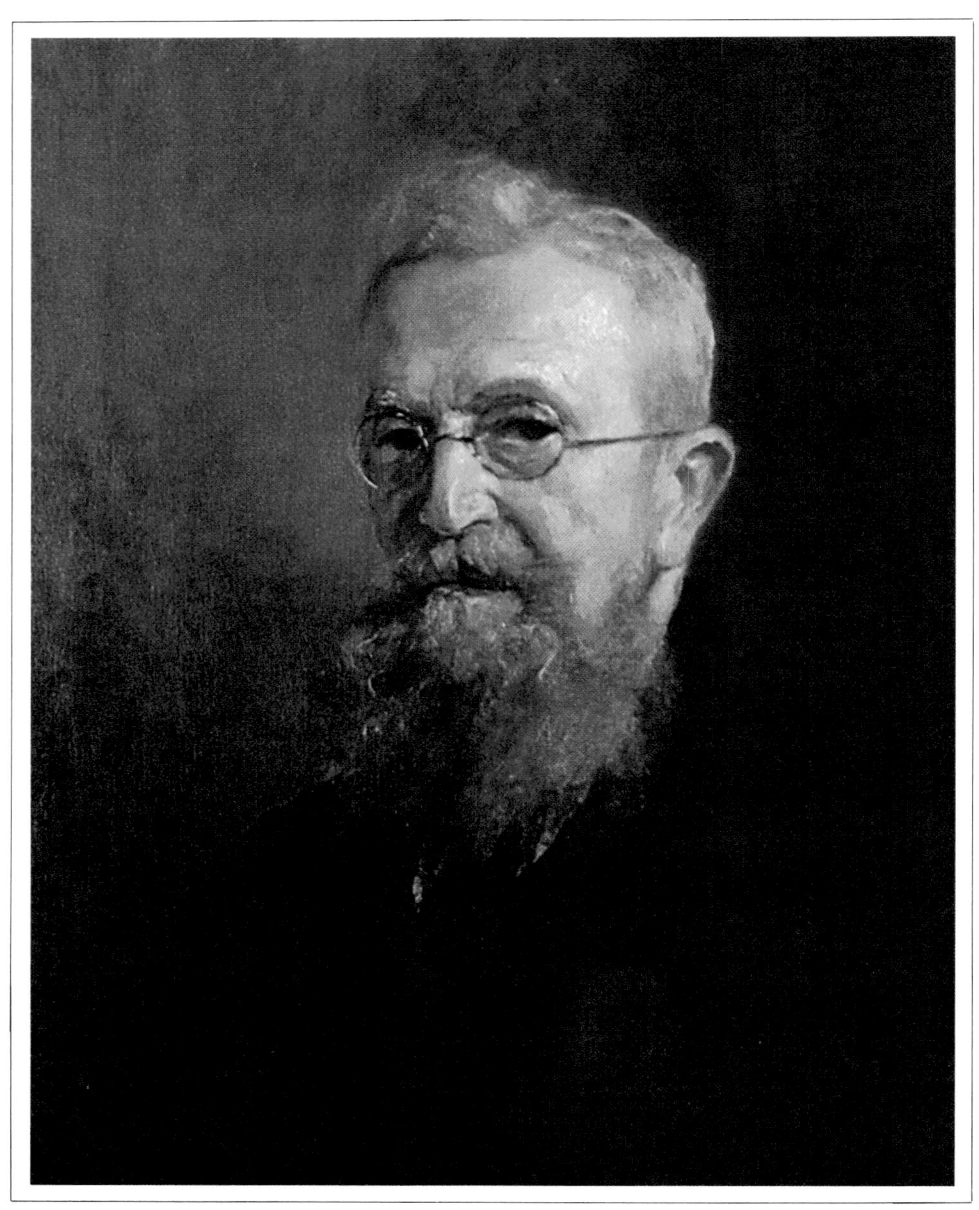

Portrait of Father Ten Boom

twenty-four

FALLING MOUNTAINS

"Therefore will not we fear, though the earth be removed, and though the mountains be carried into the midst of the sea" (Ps. 46:2).

Many mountains around us are falling. How glad I am to have the Bible, that book full of heavenly certainties that cannot be removed. We value them more when the certainties of the earth are moving as in an earthquake.

My father was always a great help to me. He was a watchmaker, but also a theologian. When I was a child I asked him one day: "Daddy, what does *predestination* mean?" He answered: "*Predestination* means that the ground on which I build my hope lies not in myself but in God's faithfulness."

Well, if we see predestination like this, it makes us glad. I have heard many predestination thoughts of the devil, who used them to take away the assurance of faith and to keep it away.

"Though the mountains be carried into the midst of the sea." The prophecies which once I did not understand are now much clearer. The things that are going to happen before Jesus will return, in the time of Antichrist, make us shudder.

It used to be all so far away; I did not understand it. Today we read the signs of the times in the newspaper. If I had never before believed the Bible, I would do so now, when I read the newspapers. When we read about wars, rumors of war, earthquakes, and other catastrophies, we can understand that people's hearts will fail them for fear. This is what the Bible also says. Terrible things are going to happen!

A pastor once said: "If I read a sad book, I always look at the last page. If I read that they find one another and live happily ever after, I read the rest with pleasure, knowing that everything will turn out well." He added, "This is what I also do with the Bible. When I feel fearful, I look at the last page. Then I know that Jesus will come again, He who promised to make all things new, so that this earth will be covered with the knowledge of the Lord, as the waters cover the bottom of the sea."

The best is yet to be. What a comfort! When things become difficult and frightening, just read the last page of the Bible. Yes, the best is yet to be! And the sufferings of this present time cannot be compared to the joys of the time that is coming. What a comfort that is!

But till then, we have this certainty in these days: "For God hath not given us the spirit of fear; but of power, and of love, and of a sound mind" (2 Tim. 1:7). The Holy Spirit causes us not to fear, even though the mountains be carried into the midst of the sea. Be filled with God's Spirit, who shows that God has no problems, only plans. There is never a panic in heaven. The Holy Spirit makes us understand the Bible. God is faithful; His plans never fail.

I remember one day when I came into a room in the concentration camp where Betsie, my sister, had a Bible study. She was telling that an architect's blueprint of a house shows all sorts of things: a threshold, a window, a roof. She said: "Just like this, God made a blueprint of your life and mine. And somewhere it said 'Ravensbrück.' God does not make any mistakes, although we do not understand Him."

Well, I most certainly did not understand when I saw Betsie starve to death. There was still so much for her to do.

One day, when we are in heaven, we shall see and understand it all. But already I sometimes see the reasons why. As for Betsie, I understand already. In my book *The Hiding Place* I tell about Betsie. And often I hear: "Your sister has been used greatly by the Lord for me. I can forgive again. She showed me that the Holy Spirit gives God's love into our hearts, and because of that even I can forgive and love my enemies." If Betsie had come out alive she might never have reached as many people as by means of the books.

Why is that book about her being used? Because, time and again, it points to the message of the Bible. Nearly everybody can obtain and read the Bible. That glorious message is in it, that God loves the world. Therefore, we need not fear, though the mountains be carried into the midst of the sea.

"God so loved the world, that he gave his only begotten Son, that whosoever believeth in him should not perish, but have everlasting life" (John 3:16). How terrible was that which happened on the cross. Surely everything was lost; what a mountain fell at that time! But just at that moment something wonderful happened, the answer to a terrible need, the need of sin. There the Savior bore the sins of the whole world—your and my sins.

Thank You, Lord, that You did this. Thank You that You finished all and that we know that You not only died for us, but that You live and are with us. And, Lord, then we shall not fear, though the earth be removed, for we shall be safe with You, whatever may happen. Hallelujah! Thank You, Lord! Amen.

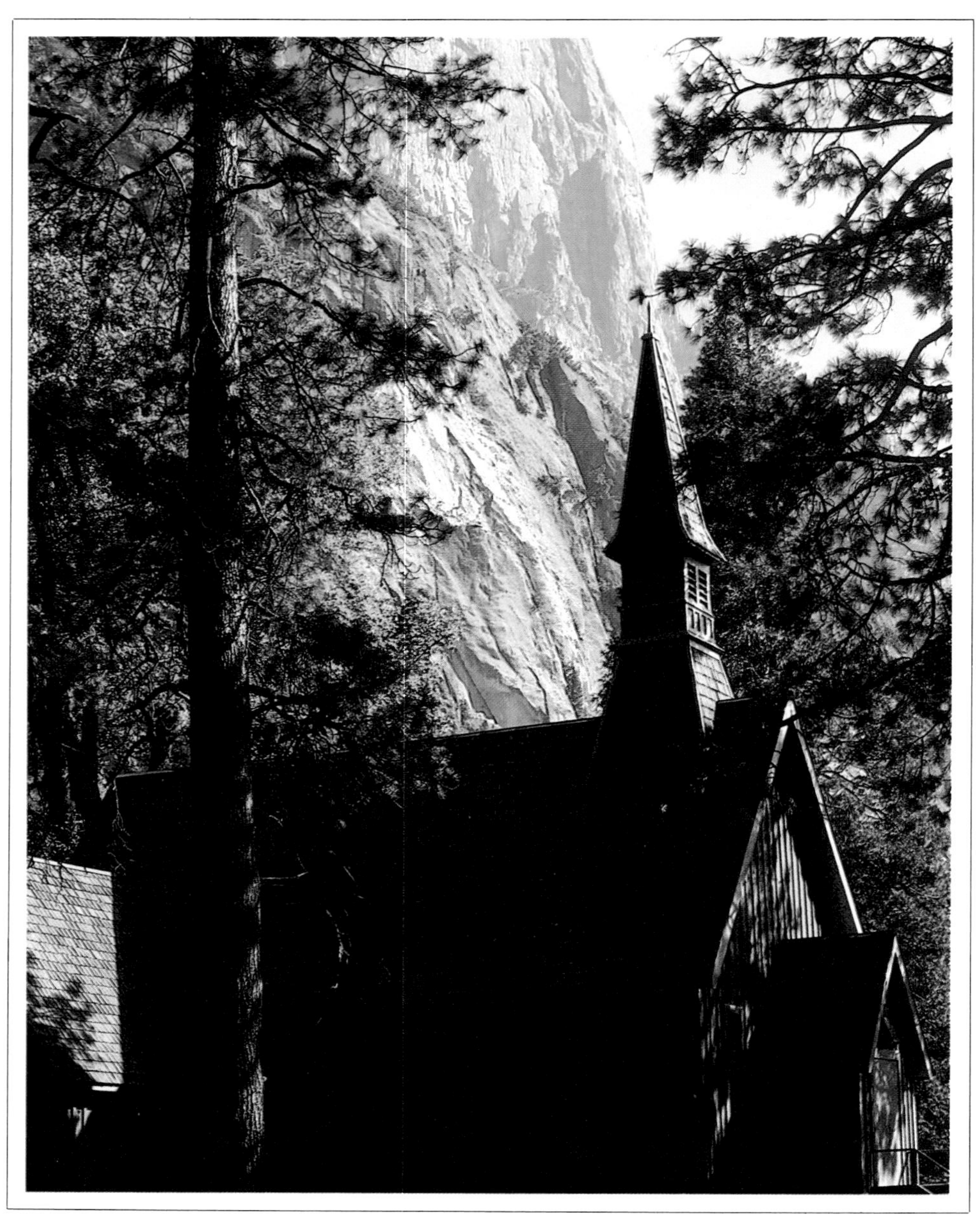

Yosemite National Park, California

twenty-five

A NEVER-FAILING EQUIPMENT FOR BATTLE

I see a clear resemblance between the life of a child of God in these days and a soldier, standing on the front line.

"Finally, my brethren, be strong in the Lord, and in the power of his might. Put on the whole armour of God, that ye may be able to stand against the wiles of the devil. For we wrestle not against flesh and blood, but against principalities, against powers, against the rulers of the darkness of this world, against spiritual wickedness in high places. Wherefore take unto you the whole armour of God, that ye may be able to withstand in the evil day, and having done all, to stand" (Eph. 6:10–13).

An army has provision officers. Imagine a soldier coming to such an officer after a battle and saying: "I could not fight; I had no guns. I was hungry, but there was nothing to eat. I saw my mate bleed to death, but I could not do anything to dress his wounds. All the time I did not know what the staff expected of me."

And an officer who had seen to everything would answer him: "But there were guns and food, which I provided. And you had the first-aid kit with the bandages."

Imagine this soldier saying: "Oh, yes, the bandages — I used them to polish my shoes." And if he said: "I never knew what I had to do," the officer might say: "I gave you a walkie-talkie, by which you could remain in constant touch with your staff." That soldier would be punished severely.

But what are we doing, if we do not use the provision of the Holy Spirit in our battle? What are our riches; what is our background? What is our provision? We have a mighty High Priest and legions of angels on our side. We have the intercession of the Lord Jesus Himself and of the Holy Spirit. "We know not what we should pray for as we ought: but the Spirit itself maketh intercession for us with groanings which cannot be uttered. . . . It is Christ that died, yea rather, that is risen again, . . . who also maketh intercession for us" (Rom. 8:26, 34). And we have the presence of the Lord Jesus, who said: "Lo, I am with you alway, even unto the end of the world" (Matt. 28:20).

He is standing at our side, in us, with us. We stand on victory ground. We have a walkie-talkie, if the Holy Spirit fills us, making our prayer a talk, a wonderful fellowship with our King.

They that are with us are much stronger than they that are against us. One day when I had to go to a place that was dangerous, I was afraid. Then somebody said to me: "When you enter, Jesus comes in." That is true, for if Jesus is in us and we are in Him, He is always with us. God's provision is perfect.

We need food, and the Bible is the bread that never gets stale. Heaven and earth shall pass away but the Word of God remains in eternity. We have the instruments, the connection with our headquarters. The Holy Spirit gives it to us by His fullness. He makes our prayers a talk with the Leader. You know, a provision officer can do much, but if the soldier does not obey, loses courage, or gets afraid, and leaves the provisions without using them, then this officer cannot help him.

I fear that when, later on, we hear God's judgment regarding our lives, we shall be ashamed because we lived as beggars. "Yes, but I was so heavy laden and I was so deeply impressed by my sins." Then the answer will be: "Heavy laden? But you had My Word: 'Come unto me, all ye that labour and are heavy laden and I will give you rest'

(Matt. 11:28). You were anxious, but I told you to cast all your care on Me. But you did not do so."

Imagine that we should say: "I could not forgive. I was so full of bitterness. To love my enemies surpassed my strength." Then the answer would be: "But you had your Bible in which it says: 'The love of God is shed abroad in our hearts by the Holy Ghost which is given to us' (Rom. 5:5). God's ocean of love was there for you personally to use every minute of day and night."

Imagine that you would say: "My sins worried me so much." Then you would hear: "Have you no Bible? Did you never read in 1 John 1: 'If we confess our sins, He is faithful and just to forgive us our sins' (v. 9) and 'the blood of Jesus Christ his Son cleanseth us from all sins' (v. 7). And 2 Corinthians 5:21: 'He hath made him to be sin for us, who knew no sin; that we might be made the righteousness of God in Him'?"

All God's promises are yes and amen in Jesus. God was serious about the promises He gave us in the Bible. Take the sword of the Spirit, the Word of God. Because of this sword we are strong and God's Word shows us that we are more than conquerors through Jesus Christ.

Lord Jesus, forgive us that so often we are discouraged because we look in the wrong direction. Teach us to accept all the riches, the strength, of Your Word, and to enjoy them that we may become Your strong, conquering soldiers. Thank You that we know that the best is yet to be. Cause us, by Your Holy Spirit, to be ashamed when we rely on ourselves and not on You. Thank You, Lord Jesus, that we can never expect too much from You. Amen.

Bible students in Birmingham, England

Springtime, a reminder of the Resurrection

Preaching in East Germany

twenty-six
VICTORY IN BATTLE

At the beginning of the last war, a boy in one of my clubs had to go into military service. He and his father had a confectioner's shop. One night he was called, along with other soldiers, to leave immediately. "There is war," they were told. He did not believe it and thought: *Another of those stupid maneuvers.* Instead of bullets, he put chocolate bars into his pouch, thinking he would comfort his comrades with these, because they had had to go out in the middle of the night. But then he learned that war had really broken out. He was lucky his superiors never heard of what he had done.

A heavy battle is coming, and perhaps it has begun already: the battle between Jesus Christ and Antichrist. And every child of God is or will be on the front line. Do we intend to fight with chocolate or with bullets? "We wrestle not against flesh and blood, but against principalities, against powers, against the rulers of the darkness of this world, against spiritual wickedness in high places" (Eph. 6:12).

Are we standing in the strength of the power of Jesus Christ? Or do we intend fighting with the chocolate bars of idealism, philosophy, humanism, or religious piety, our own endeavors and efforts? In Acts 1:8 Jesus said: "Ye shall receive power, after that the Holy Ghost is come upon you."

The armor of Ephesians 6 has no cover for the back. God cannot use deserters! "And if a man also strive for masteries, yet is he not crowned, except he strive lawfully" (2 Tim. 2:5).

On Golgotha's cross, when Jesus bore the sin of the world (your and my sins, too), He conquered the devil. There Satan went bankrupt. Jesus had twelve disciples — eleven martyrs, one deserter, a traitor. "Thou therefore endure hardness, as a good soldier of Jesus Christ" (2 Tim. 2:3), Paul wrote to Timothy.

There is power because of the Holy Spirit. The Bible tells us to be filled with God's Spirit. It is not only a matter of your having the Holy Spirit, but of the Holy Spirit's having you. The Bible is full of promises of power and victory: "more than conquerors" (Rom. 8:37); "the power of his might" (Eph. 6:10).

Now we must also live and fight as richly and strongly as we are in Jesus Christ! What do you benefit if you have a million dollars and live as a poor beggar? We must live the life that suits our wealth! A Christian's life-style must be one of victory, of joy, of abundance — a life given to us by Jesus Christ from God's fullness. We must not draw from *our* possibilities, but from *God's* possibilities; not hang on to *our* limited strength, but to *His* immeasurable strength.

The Bible speaks of putting on the new man. Conversion and new birth are needed for that. The Lord Jesus said: "Except a man be born again, he cannot see the kingdom of God" (John 3:3), and he cannot enter. We must not remain weak children of God, needing help. We must cash the checks written in the Bible to our names: inexpressible riches, love passing all understanding!

The new man must begin to live in us and he has a path to travel. Yes, but which way? Jesus Christ is *the* way. Instead of a self-centered life, there will be a God-centered life. Paul called this self-centered life the old nature. It is necessary that we come to know our old nature. That meeting is not always pleasant! To patch up our old nature is like building a nice façade, with fresh paint and clean curtains, but the interior is a ramshackle.

But he or she who wants conversion must open the door and let the

Lord Jesus enter, showing everything to Him, not hiding anything! This is called being convicted of sin, and that is something different from knowing that at times we do something wrong. He who has this meeting with Jesus and is willing to accept the consequences will find a new form of life! He puts on the new nature; he is a new creature.

Thank You, Lord Jesus, that You want to do it. I cannot do it. This old nature of mine is so tough, so strong. But it is wonderful that You will make the new nature, that You are willing to live in us by the Holy Spirit and that, therefore, we stand on victory ground in our battle with the numerous powers of darkness. Hallelujah! Amen.

Sparta, Greece

West Germany

twenty-seven

MARCHING ORDERS FOR THE CHURCH

"Thou therefore endure hardness, as a good soldier of Jesus Christ" (2 Tim. 2:3). A soldier must know the instructions. Commandments are the rules of the game. King Jesus said: "As my Father hath sent me, even so send I you" (John 20:21). We can know the rules of the game when we read Jesus' actions in the Bible.

A soldier must obey. Much in our lives gets broken because it is not according to God's plan, God's purpose. To sin means to miss the mark.

In the Old Testament we read that God came to live in the tabernacle because this was built according to His will. What is the goal of our battles? The goal is a future where this earth will be covered with the knowledge of the Lord as the waters cover the bottom of the sea. Here on this earth a change of throne will take place, from the prince of darkness to the King of Light. The prince of this world, the prince of darkness, will be dethroned and Jesus, the King, the Prince of Light, the Messiah, will reign.

In order to be allowed to serve in the army of the King of Kings, we must come just as we are, with all our sinfulness, our lack of freedom, our ignorance. But we do not remain as we are. The King Himself sees to it that we shall be trained and receive an armor in our battles against sin, which will bring us to victory ground. We do not need to make it, we only must put it on. It is God's armor. Read about it in Ephesians 6:10–20.

Your ties to the past, to people, to habits, all will the Lord break in order that you may be really free. Jesus says in John 8:36: "If the Son therefore shall make you free, ye shall be free indeed." Your inability He will change into ability, so that you will cry out: "I can do all things through Christ which strengtheneth me" (Phil. 4:13).

How is that possible? By opening all the doors and windows and drawers and purses to the Lord Jesus. When you opened the curtains this morning, your room suddenly was filled with light. Just like that, the Holy Spirit is ready to come in wherever the doors are opened. That commandment, the wonderful, most joyful commandment of the Bible to be filled with the Spirit, will become a reality all of a sudden. Jesus wants to live in us through His Spirit.

Then the fruit of the Spirit and the gifts of the Spirit will appear and be at your disposal. Read it in Galatians 5:22–23 and 1 Corinthians 12–14. Chapter 13 speaks of God's love that has been "shed abroad in our hearts by the Holy Ghost which is given unto us" (Rom. 5:5). This love is different from human love. That love will fail in the long run, but God's love will never fail.

What armor do we possess when we enter the army of King Jesus? Do you realize that you cannot do it, that I cannot do it, that it is Jesus alone who, in spite of everything, has power already and who makes us more than conquerors, because He comes to live in us by His Spirit?

But why then do you often feel alone? You feel as if you were far away, as if you stood alone in the battle — just like a soldier who has to go reconnoitering and feels in danger; he trembles because he lost the liaison with the rest of the army and the staff. Such a soldier needs a walkie-talkie, which keeps him in touch with his superiors, so that he can consult them all the time.

Our King never sends us to the front line without a walkie-talkie. We have a wonderful, continual contact with Him in prayer. "Pray without ceasing" (1 Thess. 5:17), the Bible says. That does not mean that we have to be on our knees all the time, but it means the unceasing connection with the Master, especially in the battle of daily life. Sometimes it is just a sigh, sometimes an exclamation: "Lord, I thank You that You are with me"; "Lord, help me, things are so hard"; "I acted wrongly, Lord, will You forgive and help me that I shall not do it again?"; "Lord, I thank You and praise You. You are taking care of me in such a wonderful way." In this way the Master will make you more than conqueror.

Master, will You repair our walkie-talkies of prayer, wherever it is needed? You are the Author and Finisher of our faith. Will You make it a real conversation, when we are alone with You, but also amidst all the things of everyday life? Listen, Lord, to those who say: "I put my hand in Yours, Lord. Together with You, I am more than conqueror." Amen.

Canada

twenty-eight

GOD'S MYSTERIES AND OUR FAITHFULNESS

In 1 Corinthians 4:1–2 Paul speaks of "ministers of Christ, and stewards of the mysteries of God. Moreover it is required in stewards, that a man be found faithful."

First of all we must know what the mysteries of God are. Well, we can read about them in the Bible. God has revealed them to us. We shall understand many of the mysteries after opening our hearts to the Lord Jesus. He reveals them to us through His Spirit and then we have to pass them on!

One is: "For God so loved the world, that He gave His only begotten Son, that whosoever believeth in him should not perish, but have everlasting life" (John 3:16).

If we accept such a tremendous mystery of God, we have to pass it on. We must be faithful regarding this truth and many others. It makes us happy and thankful to know such a mystery. And what does God then expect of us? Well, that we are faithful, that is all. Love and obedience belong together.

But our task is no small thing! Paul says: "We are ambassadors for Christ, as though God did beseech you by us: . . . be ye reconciled to God" (2 Cor. 5:20). And Jesus said to the Father: "As thou hast sent me . . . even so have I also sent them" (John 17:18). This means in fact that every believer is a missionary.

Is that possible? Yes. "God hath not given us the spirit of fear; but of power, and of love, and of a sound mind" (2 Tim. 1:7). We do not need to draw from our own resources; we can draw from God's resources. We do not need to count on our own limited strength; we can count on God's boundless strength.

Is every believer, even if he or she has an ordinary task — factory hand, tradesman, housewife — really a steward of God's mysteries?

Three men were once laying bricks. A passerby asked the first one: "What are you doing?"

"I am building a wall."

He asked the next one, who said: "I am earning a living for my wife and children."

The third one said: "I am building a cathedral."

Every believer is building God's kingdom, whether he or she is a watchmaker, a bricklayer, a housewife, or a professor.

A calling can make you very original. Some time ago I talked with a coal merchant. He told me that he had two telephones standing next to each other on his desk. "Often I have a call on each line," he said. "On one I tell of the Lord Jesus and give spiritual help, often while, on the other, somebody is ordering coal. Then both can hear what I say, because I ask the second person to wait a minute and so he, too, hears the gospel. After that I ask: 'How much coal do you want?'"

This was what he considered being a steward of God's mysteries — a believer being steward of God's mysteries and of a coal trade at the same time.

God only demands that we are faithful. Faithful! And it is wonderful that even in this faithfulness we do not need to summon in our own strength. In Galatians 5:22–23 something is said about the fruit of the Spirit, and faithfulness also is part of it. We do it together: He and we.

Paul says: "If we believe not, yet he abideth faithful: he cannot deny himself" (2 Tim. 2:13). This faithfulness endures forever and ever!

If we walk hand in hand with Jesus, we remain faithful and we can continue to be conscious of our calling even if everything seems dark and lost.

The Lord says: "He that believeth on me, the works that I do shall he do also; and greater works than these shall he do; because I go unto my Father" (John 14:12).

Is that possible? Greater works than Jesus did? You? I?

Yes, for Jesus is at the right hand of the Father, and He is doing greater works *now* than He did during the three-and-one-half years in Palestine. But He is doing them through His followers, you and me. And this is how He makes us stewards of God's mysteries.

Thank You, Lord Jesus, that You have such wonderful work for us. Thank You that You are willing to use us and that You can do so because You, Lord, fight together with Your disciples and because You constantly give to us from Your supplies: faithfulness, love, strength, and courage, through Your Holy Spirit. Amen.

twenty-nine

WHO IS RESPONSIBLE?

A child of God must surrender to our heavenly Father and has the privilege of doing so many times.

The beginning is to be born as a child of God. The Lord Jesus calls this "new birth." The Bible says: "As many as received him, to them gave he power to become the sons of God" (John 1:12). "As ye have therefore received Christ Jesus the Lord, so walk ye in him" (Col. 2:6).

Someone said to me: "I have surrendered several times to the Lord—again a little while ago, during a conference. I felt so happy. But it only lasted a short time and everything was gone again."

If this is your experience, you must change the direction of your look. You looked at yourself, and you could not persevere. Look at the Lord to whom you surrendered.

If God began the work of your complete surrender and if God accepted your surrender, then He will take care of you and hold you. Do you believe this?

In the matter of complete surrender, two are involved: God and I. I am nothing at all. God is the eternal and almighty Lord. Are you afraid to entrust yourself to this powerful Savior? God wants to do His part. Don't you think He can hold you, moment by moment, day by day? God makes the sun shine every day, even though it is sometimes hidden behind the clouds. Can't God likewise let His life shine on you and me,

India

Uganda

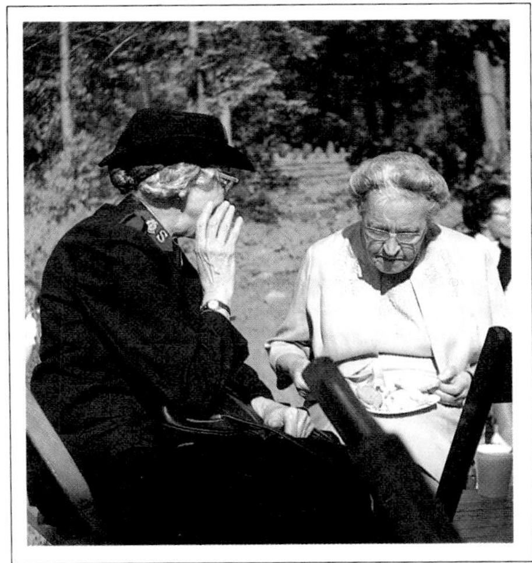

United States

Lweza, Uganda

moment by moment, day by day, without interruption? Why did you not experience this? Because you did not trust Him.

A life of surrender does have difficulties. It is not only difficult, it is impossible for men to persevere. But by God's grace, by the power of the Holy Spirit, who lives in you, it is *this* life to which we are called and—praise the Lord!—He can and will persevere.

Did you ever hear of George Müller? On his ninetieth birthday he was asked the secret of his continuous joy and happiness. He answered: "There are two things. One is that by the grace of God I have had a good conscience day by day. The other is that I have so much loved the Word of God, the Bible." This is a good description of a surrendered life: a good conscience because of obedience to the Lord day by day in His strength and mercy, and fellowship with the Lord through reading the Bible and in prayer.

We must be willing to do what God wants us to do. The other requirement is letting God do what *He* wants to do.

Surrender to God's will. You don't always know what that is, but then just say: "By Your mercy I want to do Your will in all things, every minute of every day. May no word I say be without Your glory, no activity apart from Your glory, everything according to Your blessed will."

Is this possible? What did God promise? "Eye hath not seen, nor ear heard, neither have entered into the heart of man, the things which God hath prepared for them that love him" (1 Cor. 2:9). His blessings surpass your imagination—divine riches.

I want you to say and to do something. Say: "I surrender completely to the Lord and His will, to do only His will." God Himself will enable you to work out your surrender.

Then say: "I surrender completely to the Lord that He may work in me, and live in me according to His good pleasure, as He promised." Only through surrender to the Lord Jesus can we know true freedom.

Yes, God wants to work in His children in a way we cannot understand. And He wants to do this every day, every moment. We only have to trust Him as a child does.

Who is responsible? Ahab said to his enemy Benhadad: "My lord, O king, . . . I am thine, and all that I have" (1 Kin. 20:4).

If we say this to God, His blessing comes upon us; He accepts us and will teach us what it means.

When you pour tea, you use a clean, empty cup. If the cup has ink or vinegar in it, you cannot use it.

God will fill us and bless us, if we give ourselves completely to Him and are emptied of ourselves.

There was a time when so many responsibilities came to me that they nearly frightened me. So many meetings, so much traveling and more and more different kinds of work—great opportunities, but oppressing. I was not as strong as ten years before.

So I told everything to the Lord. How wonderful it is that He understands us better than we do ourselves! Then the Lord asked me: "Did you surrender completely to Me?"

I could answer: "Yes, Lord, a hundred percent."

"Do you know that then you do not possess anything any more, that you are just a steward of that which you have? This means that I am responsible. You only must obey Me and follow Me and then I am your victory, your strength, your all."

I knew what God meant. I remembered the time when I was alone in a prison cell, owning nothing but the clothes I was wearing. Life before I was imprisoned had been very hard. We were responsible for hundreds of Jews, hiding with many families. We had to take care of food, hospitals, funerals, and hundreds of other things. When I was there all alone, one day the thought came: *I do not possess anything. I cannot do anything, but neither have I any responsibility.*

Other underground workers during the war experienced this when, after dangerous and strenuous, but often successful, work to save Jewish children and adults, they suddenly found themselves alone in a cell and could no longer do anything. It was not voluntary, just like Ahab who was in Benhadad's power. But I understood what it meant to possess nothing and not to have any responsibility.

When the Lord asked me whether I had given all to Him, it was quite different. It was a blessed, altogether glorious surrender into His loving hands. Then I knew that not *I* but *He* had all responsibility. This gave me such rest and peace. Suddenly I saw how dynamic is surrender to the Lord. *His* ability, *His* omnipotence, *His* perfect insight and discernment, *His* love are so much greater than what I, in my short-sightedness, had considered my duty—to do all this work in *my* strength, *my* ability.

Now *my* strength, *my* ability are no longer reckoned with. Everything depends on *His* ability, *His* power.

Suddenly I saw Gideon, weak and afraid. But the angel said to him: "The LORD is with thee, thou mighty man of valour" (Judg. 6:12). Because the Lord was with him, He was a strong hero.

I was so happy after this talk with the Lord that I said to Him: "O Lord, I should so much love to see You."

The Lord answered: "Look at your left hand."

And then I saw that my hand was in another hand and that this hand was pierced. How safe!

No longer I, but He, in me: Jesus, crucified but also risen, also glorified. He, in me; I, in Him.

We must not try to understand this. It is incomprehensible, but so safe. Hand in hand with Jesus. Just walk with Him. He is Victor, and He wants to make you and me more than conquerors. Hallelujah, what a Savior!

Lord, I thank You that it does not depend on me, but on You. I trust You to be willing to live in me, to hold me and to make me strong in a life lived to Your honor. Lord, listen now to those who say this with me. You see, Lord, who is reading this and saying with me: Take my life completely. Amen.

thirty
TAKE STOCK

During the years I had a watchmaker's business at Haarlem, I had the habit of taking stock at the end of the year. I liked to do this.

Now I want to try to take stock of the supplies we as God's children have. This really is an impossible thing and however much we work, it always encompasses only a small part of what we really have. But it is useful. When we are in Christ it is necessary that we learn to live as rich people, for the world is poor.

Once I heard somebody review the first four days of the new year. There were many fearful events to report, and his last words were: "I tremble to think of the rest of the year." And many people all over the world shared this feeling with him.

A Christian can and must be realistic. In our days we see Antichrist marching on. When we read the Bible regarding the current happenings and those we must expect before Jesus comes again, we can expect times of tension.

In Luke 21 the Lord Jesus warned us and showed us the way with respect to all the things that are happening now. We can expect terrible things, also persecution. But the Lord says: "Be not terrified: for these things must first come to pass. . . . there shall not an hair of your head perish. . . . lift up your heads; for your redemption draweth nigh" (vv. 9, 18, 28).

At one time I was in a country where persecution broke out. Christians were killed. All of a sudden a deep joy welled up in me. Never had I opened the Bible with such thankfulness. I read Romans 8 and 1 Peter 1. What wonderful abundance for the children of God in need!

We are all more or less on the front line of the battle, not against flesh and blood, but against the spiritual wickedness, against principalities, against the rulers of the darkness of this world. It is a battle that will be increasingly heavy and severe and in which we shall need the armor of God, as described in Ephesians 6, very much.

I once heard that a person gave the advice that we as Christians should learn Morse code. Then, if we were imprisoned it would be very useful. Well, I cannot agree. When during the war I was in prison, I knew the Morse code, but it did not help me very much. What was valuable to me was every Bible text and every hymn I knew by heart. Learning these by heart is a preparation we can all have.

You need not necessarily begin with Genesis 1 or Matthew 1, but ask the Lord to guide you by His Holy Spirit in the choice of Bible verses.

Yes, we must learn to handle the sword of God, even if we should not have the Bible any more. What vision Romans 8 gives us! The suffering of this time cannot be compared with the glory that is coming. Maybe you see threats and death around you, but a far greater reality is that Jesus lives and is with us. "Whom having not seen, ye love" (1 Peter 1:8).

Especially in days of tribulation we shall be used. We can argue about the tribulation and the rapture of the believers, but in tribulation we can be strong, by taking the promises of the Bible seriously.

Already in a large part of the world, God's children are being persecuted. In our time there is darkness all over the world, and we know about the needs of the world. There is fear because of the uncertainty of all the visible things. But Romans says: "The whole creation groaneth and travaileth in pain together until now. And not only they, but ourselves also, which have the firstfruits of the Spirit. . . . For the earnest expectation of the creature waiteth for the manifestation of the sons of God" (Rom. 8:22–23, 19).

Who are these? "For as many as are led by the Spirit of God, they are the sons of God" (Rom. 8:14).

What does the groaning creation see when it looks at you and me? Does it see beggars, poor and miserable beings, or does it see children of the King? Eva von Tiele Winckler once said: "We are the children of a King, and we have the keys to the treasure room of our Father. These treasures are available to us every moment of the day."

I am only just at the beginning of the supplies of this treasure room.

Lord Jesus, will You forgive us when we live like beggars, although You suffered on the cross in order to make us rich children of a King? Holy Spirit, open our eyes. Give us vision that we may know how rich we are and that the groaning creation may see in us that which it so greatly desires: victorious, relaxed, rich children of God. Help us to make the world jealous, in a holy way, to receive the peace that passeth all understanding. Amen.

thirty-one

ARE YOU READY FOR JESUS' RETURN?

In Luke 21:36 we read: "Watch ye therefore, and pray always, that ye may be accounted worthy to escape all these things that shall come to pass, and to stand before the Son of man."

You can be ready, even if Jesus would come again today.

How is that possible? We find the answer in the Bible, and we shall read it together.

I know there are people who say: "Many people believed that Jesus would come soon. But they died meanwhile, and Jesus did not return."

Jesus told us to watch the signs of the times, and talk like this is a sign of the times. Peter said: "Knowing this first, that there shall come in the last days scoffers, walking after their own lusts, and saying, Where is the promise of his coming?" (2 Peter 3:3–4).

Talking like that is a sign that we are in the last days, because the speaker is a scoffer, who does not long for Jesus' return. When we are placed before the Son of Man, our own desires can be a real stumbling block. Perhaps you say: "I have not gotten this far yet." You will of course understand that Jesus will not wait till everybody has gotten this far.

He will come, and there will be a moment that everyone will bow before Him, everyone — whether he has gotten this far or not. Then the matter will be whether you will bow your knees before your Savior or before your Judge. The Lord Jesus Himself warned us.

He longs for us to be ready, and therefore He says: "Watch ye therefore, and pray always, that ye may be accounted worthy to escape all these things that shall come to pass, and to stand before the Son of man" (Luke 21:36).

The most evident sign is that the Jews returned to their country. But there are other signs of the times. Knowledge will increase. How much knowledge we have in our days! We even know on earth when there is a moonquake because of the seismograph we humans put on the moon.

"He that is unjust, let him be unjust still: and he which is filthy, let him be filthy still: and he that is righteous, let him be righteous still: and he that is holy, let him be holy still" (Rev. 22:11). Everything is escalating. I never met so many dedicated young Christians as now, who are willing to live for Jesus and, if necessary, to die for Him. But neither did I ever see or read and hear about so much filthy impurity as now.

But enough about the signs of the times. The question now is: How can we be prepared?

Philippians 1:9–11 says: "And this I pray, that your love may abound yet more and more in knowledge and in all judgment; that ye may approve things that are excellent; that ye may be sincere and without offence till the day of Christ; being filled with the fruits of righteousness, which are by Jesus Christ, unto the glory and praise of God."

Is that possible? Love, so abundant in your and my heart? We shall never be able to love like this.

No, you and I can't, but the Holy Spirit can. Read Romans 5:1–11. Verses 5–6 say: "Hope maketh not ashamed; because the love of God is shed abroad in our hearts by the Holy Ghost which is given unto us. For when we were yet without strength, in due time Christ died for the ungodly." Being now justified by His blood, we shall be saved from wrath *through Him.*

The Holy Spirit has been given to us. Does the Holy Spirit have you? Then you will be filled. He is willing to fill you, just as the light filled your room when you opened the curtains. The Lord Jesus wants to live in your heart and life through His Holy Spirit. If only the door of your sitting room is open, then you will not experience His victory in your office or in the kitchen.

Some people think that complete surrender is only possible for those who are in full-time gospel work — missionaries, pastors, ministers. But everyone can and must be ready for Jesus' return. Everyone can live in complete surrender to the Lord — you, too.

John says: "And now, little children, abide in him; that, when he shall appear, we may have confidence, and not be ashamed before him at his coming" (1 John 2:28).

At this moment Jesus is knocking at the door of your heart. Are you willing to say, "Yes, Lord, come into my heart?" Then He will come and prepare you for His return. He longs for you, He loves you. He longs more for us to be ready than we ourselves long for and want it. In John 15:5, He said: "He that abideth in me, and I in him, the same bringeth forth much fruit." You cannot prepare yourself for Jesus' return: "Without me ye can do nothing."

But stop compromising. In your heart there is a cross and a throne. If your ego is on the throne, then Jesus is on the cross. If Jesus is on the throne, then your ego is on the cross.

And He, Jesus, will establish you until the end, that you may be unblameable on the day of our Lord Jesus Christ. What a Savior!

Lord Jesus, thank You that You are changing me from within, that You are willing to do so in each one who now says, "Yes, Lord Jesus, come into my heart, fill me with Your Spirit, prepare me for Your return. Take my life." How wonderful, Lord, that You will do it! Hallelujah! Amen.

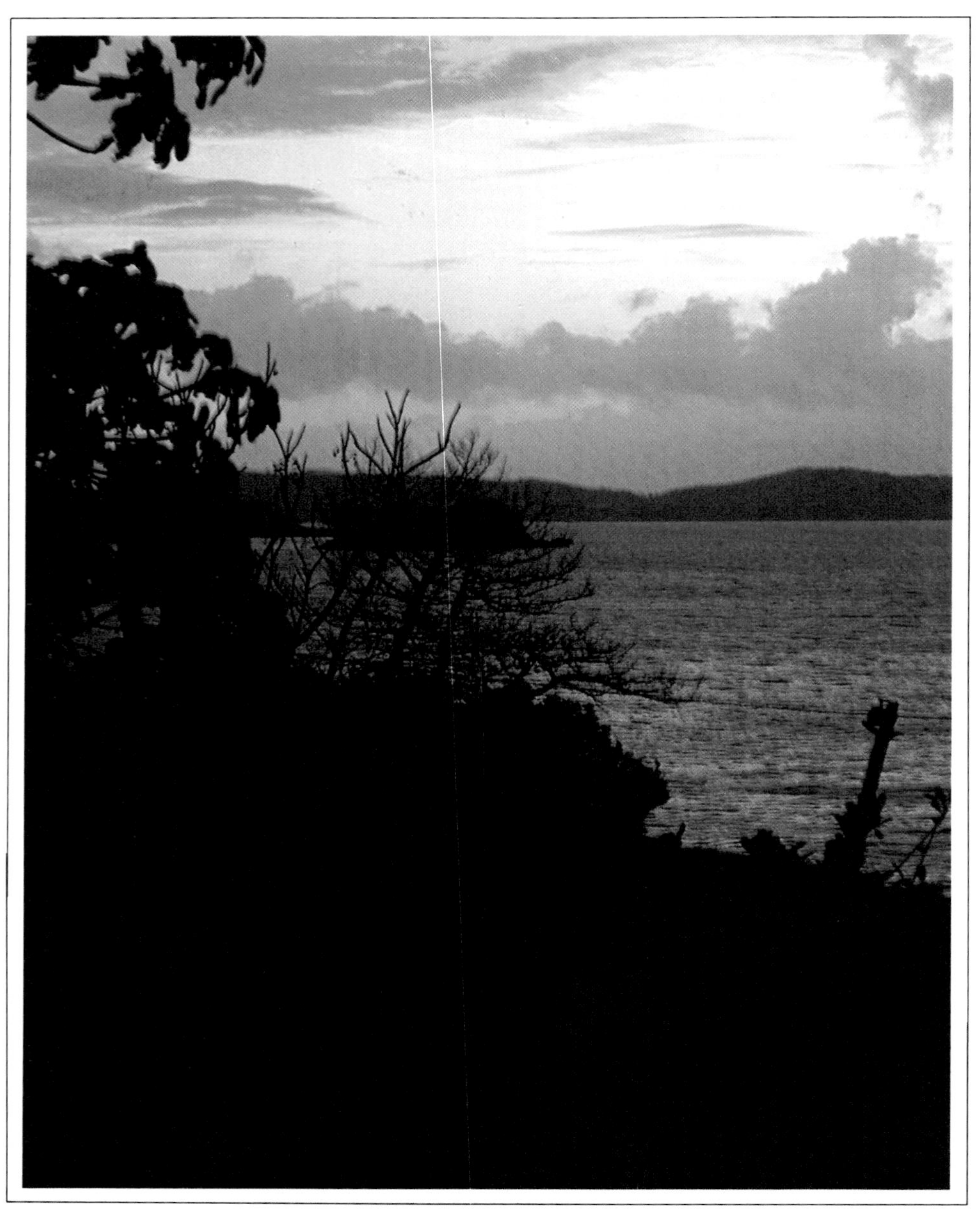

Bermuda

thirty-two

WHEN GOD SAYS, "WAIT"

Are you ever discouraged because of an unanswered prayer? How often we think when a prayer is not answered that God has said no. Many times He has simply said, "Wait." Never doubt that God hears our prayers, even the unusual ones.

When God says, "No" or "Wait," it is because He knows what we do not know. He sees His side of the embroidery all the time. One day we will see the same side as He does. Thank Him for every answered and unanswered prayer. To those who love God, all things work together for good.

I thank all of you who have prayed for the return of my speech after my stroke. God has not fully answered this prayer yet (my coworker Pam is helping me to write), but I know that in this too, He is working for good. All our times are in His hands and that includes the "whys?" and the "whens?" and the "how longs?"

Once when looking up some old papers, I found a letter I had written in 1944 while in solitary confinement. At that time I was surrounded by cruelty; now I am surrounded by people who love and help me. Even so, there are some aspects of my present condition that remind me of the isolation of those prison days.

Dear ones, I have asked the Lord to bring me out of this prison. He answered: "My grace is sufficient for you." I looked to Him and tried not to be impatient. I know that I will be here not one minute longer than God thinks necessary for me. I can wait for His time. I have adjusted myself to the lonesome life, but I am not really alone, for I have such a blessed fellowship with the Lord. I talk much with my Savior. I receive a deeper insight into time and eternity. I am ready to live and ready to die. ". . . having a desire to depart, and to be with Christ; which is far better" (Phil. 1:23).

I had a problem with my worry about Father and Betsie. But I talked it over with the Lord and He said: "They are hidden in My immensely great love." After that I had no worry about them any more.

My Savior takes away all my homesickness, so that the doctor said to me: "You are always so good-humored." Indeed, I have so much to be thankful for. There is inside me a real song of praise. The fellowship with the Lord is so joyful that I am even thankful to be alone. Just imagine! You know how fond I am of fellowship with other people!

I see my sins clearer than before — my ego and much superficiality. It is a miracle that I can adjust so well to this life and that I am so happy. Often it is dark, but then my Savior gives me His light and what a joy that is. Soon we will meet again in God's time. Your loving Corrie.

Indeed, God gives grace for whatever is happening in our lives. At that time He helped me to be alone and without any activity. And He helps me now in the limitations of my physical condition.

Lord Jesus, Your grace is indeed sufficient for our needs. Help us to trust You and be content whatever our circumstances. Thank you, Lord. Amen.

thirty-three

PRAISE AND OBEDIENCE

God seeks our praise whatever our circumstances. I am reminded of a story about the famous conductor, Sir Michael Costa. As he was conducting a rehearsal with hundreds of instruments and voices, the mighty chorus rang out with the thunder of the organ, the roll of drums, and the blare of horns. In the midst of all the din, one man who played the piccolo, far up in a corner, said to himself, "It does not matter what I do," and ceased to play.

Suddenly, the great conductor stopped, flung up his hands, and quieted the performers. "Where is the piccolo?" he cried. His sharp ear had missed it, and the whole piece had been spoiled.

What about you? You may be insignificant and hidden, yet God seeks your praise. He listens for it, and all the music of the great universe is made richer and sweeter because you give Him your best.

In one of the meetings I once held with students, we had listened together to the Holy Spirit and His word about victory. We experienced the reality of God's promise to us that we can be conquerors of weakness and fear in our lives. One of the boys said to me, "Now there are no problems left. I see the answer to all my questions and know that there will not be an unsolvable problem in the future." I could understand him and was able to share with him that such riches give a foretaste of heavenly joy. I also told him that in order to have the total picture we need to realize that faith is a battle (see Eph. 6:12). Therefore, we need the whole armor of God.

The Bible tells us that dark powers are conquered enemies, and I see in this fight described in Ephesians 6 a very real battle of faith. Our strength in this battle comes from the Holy Spirit who has been given to us. When we open our hearts to Him, He is willing to fill us. And then, instead of the powers of darkness, there comes into our hearts the fruit of the Spirit—love, joy, peace, patience, kindness, goodness, faithfulness, gentleness, and self-control. For us the solving of the sin problem is not to try to pull out the root of sin; the answer is the indwelling of the Holy Spirit. Jesus prayed to the Father to give us this Comforter ". . . that he may abide with you for ever; even the Spirit of truth . . ." (John 14:16–17).

I visited a friend of mine in Holland who is the happy father of eight children. In the attic I saw eight beds. I asked him, "Why in the world did you not buy a house with bedrooms for your children?" "I have," my friend said, "but there is a family in my house who will not leave. When they leave, all my children get their own bedrooms!"

My friend had bought and paid for the house, yet he had to wait to gain full possession. Jesus has bought us with His blood. He suffered terribly at the cross. He has a legal right to fill us with His joy if we have accepted Him as our Lord and Savior. "These things I have spoken unto you, that my joy might remain in you . . ." (John 15:11). But where our ego lives, He cannot enter.

Thank You, Lord Jesus, for dying on the cross to redeem us and to cleanse us from sin. Thank You, Holy Spirit, for living within us and teaching us the truth about ourselves and about God. Father, we commit our lives to You. Amen.

Uganda

Lweza, Uganda

— *thirty-four* —
SUMMER 1977

Surely my life has changed. But don't call it retirement! I must tell you that it is more like getting "new tires." My life is no less productive, but it is different.

I don't travel any more. My career as a tramp for the Lord has ended as far as I can understand, and my work is now writing books and making messages for films, which will reach perhaps more people than I reached with my talks in meetings.

I am enjoying this life immensely. I now have time to study, to read, and to write my books without interruption. I am living in California and enjoying the climate and the little garden I have here.

Once when I was in solitary confinement, I was called out to be questioned. Going from the building where the cells were, I had to cross a square to a small building where people underwent interrogation and were tortured. While walking across the square, I saw some tiny white flowers. Shepherd's-purse was growing between the bricks used in the construction of the square.

When the guard who accompanied me looked the other way, I bent down and picked some of those little flowers and tucked them in the bosom of my dress. When back in my cell, I took a broken medicine bottle, arranged my "bouquet," and put it behind my cup so that the guards could not see it when they looked through the peephole in my door. That tiny bouquet was my garden, and I enjoyed it as the only nice thing in the cell.

Now I have a garden with little lemon and orange trees, and I enjoy them every moment I work outside or sit on one of my garden chairs, which some dear people gave me at a "patio shower." I am surrounded by beauty and love.

"I have learned, in whatsoever state I am, therewith to be content. I know both how to be abased, and I know how to abound: every where and in all things I am instructed both to be full and to be hungry, both to abound and to suffer need. I can do all things through Christ which strengtheneth me" (Phil. 4:11–13).

I was ready to accept my poor little bouquet of six blades of grass and three little flowers as my garden because of Him who was in me, and I could say then with Paul when he wrote from his prison to the Philippians, "I count all things but loss for the excellency of the knowledge of Christ Jesus my Lord: for whom I have suffered the loss of all things, and do count them but dung, that I may win Christ" (Phil. 3:8).

Yes, I know how to abound and I know how to be poor. "Brethren, I count not myself to have apprehended: but this one thing I do, forgetting those things which are behind, and reaching forth to those things which are before, I press toward the mark for the prize of the high calling of God in Christ Jesus" (Phil. 3:13–14).

Thank You, Lord, that You strengthen us to do Your will, no matter what our circumstances. Holy Spirit, fill us with the zeal Paul had to count all things loss for the sake of knowing You. Amen.

thirty-five

WILL YOU SEE JESUS?

In the jungle of Vietnam, I had a talk with a chief one day. His name is Tsau. For a week I had been speaking to his tribe, and he thanked me on behalf of his tribesmen. He gave me the title of "Double-old Grandmother." In the Tsjill tribe and in other tribes of Vietnam, old age is a great honor. He continued, saying: "You came a long distance, a very long distance. You are old, very old. You had to travel a long way in order to come here and tell us about the Lord Jesus. Will you thank your tribe that they let you go in order to come here?"

He gave me a copper bracelet. That was the sign of a treaty with his tribe. Such a sign is given when tribes become reconciled, when a large debt is paid off completely, and when two people marry. "With you," Tsau said, "it is a prayer treaty. We shall pray for you, you will pray for us, and in the future we shall belong together."

Then I asked him: "Have you a message for my tribe in Holland?"

After thinking this over, he said: "Tell them that, if a person does not repent of his sins, he will not see Jesus when He comes again."

That is the message I now pass on to you, in the name of the Tsjill tribe and Tsau, their chief. We do not know at what time or on which day Jesus will come again, but neither do we know of a day or an hour when He cannot come. If He should come today, could you look into His eyes?

It is a wonderful thing that we can all be ready. If we confess our sins, Jesus will forgive us and cleanse us with His blood. A heart that has

Overleaf: West Germany

been cleansed by Him, He will fill with His Holy Spirit. The Spirit will work such wonderful things in us that we shall be ready. It is a matter of surrender to Him. The Bible says: "He which hath begun a good work in you will perform it until the day of Jesus Christ" (Phil. 1:6).

I was with American soldiers, near the front line at Danang. Can you imagine what it meant to them that an old lady came to see them? Their wives and mothers were far away in America. One of them said: "She smiles just like my grandmother." I felt like a grandmother with these boys, who were in great danger of their lives.

At first I made them laugh heartily. Americans have a great sense of humor. But then I spoke to them very seriously. "Boys," I said, "we all know that you are in danger of your lives. It is possible that tomorrow you will be killed. Are you ready to look a righteous God in the eyes? It is possible if you repent and take your sins to Jesus. He wants to forgive you and to cleanse your heart with His blood and fill it with His Spirit. He said: 'Come to Me: and him that cometh to me I will in no wise cast out' [John 6:37]." Many of these boys and men came. It is quite possible that now they are in heaven.

What about you who are reading this? Perhaps you will say: I am not on the front line of a war; my life is not in danger. But we all know that every person will have to die one day and after that the judgment—everyone, whether he wants it or not. Are you ready? Are you ready for Jesus to come again? If so, that is great, but you must use your time to show the way to others.

Every person has an eternity to gain or lose. And when we know Jesus, we also know the way. Then we must tell others that He is the way, the truth, and the life. Tell many people. Let us work as long as it is day, you in your corner and I in mine.

If the Lord calls you to a place far from home, go! If you have to stay where you are, be obedient, for God can use us only in the place where He calls us.

Is it not wonderful to work for a King who never has lost one battle?

Thank You, Lord Jesus, that we know that You will return to this earth. Show us that we must repent of our sins in order to see You when You come again. Holy Spirit, make us feel disturbed if there is one unconfessed sin left in our life and heart. Thank You, Lord Jesus, that on the cross You bore the sins of the whole world — my sins and the sins of those who are praying now. Amen.

Tucson, Arizona

Jan 1st 45 Corrie is free & goes 2 Berlin then on 2 Holland. 53yrs old

May 5 Liberation Day of Holland

" 8 VE DAY in Europe.

June 19 C writes 2 the man who betrayed them. forgives him

1947 C is in Germany: she meets guard from Camp & " "

1954 C meets nurse who was bad 2 Betsie in Camp leads her 2 the Lord.

1959 C goes back 2 Ravensbruck & find out she was let out by error

1962 C is made a knight in the Order.

1975 the movie The Hiding Place is started

1983 C dies aged 91. dies on April 15 her birthday.

1988 April 15 Corrie Ten Boom house opens as a museum.